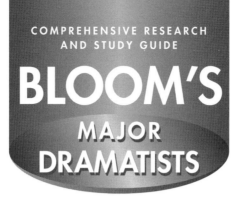

COMPREHENSIVE RESEARCH
AND STUDY GUIDE

BLOOM'S

MAJOR
DRAMATISTS

*Oscar
Wilde*

EDITED AND WITH AN
INTRODUCTION BY HAROLD BLOOM

BLOOM'S MAJOR DRAMATISTS

Aeschylus

Anton Chekhov

Aristophanes

Berthold Brecht

Euripides

Henrik Ibsen

Ben Jonson

Christopher Marlowe

Arthur Miller

Eugene O'Neill

Shakespeare's Comedies

Shakespeare's Histories

Shakespeare's Romances

Shakespeare's Tragedies

George Bernard Shaw

Neil Simon

Sophocles

Tennessee Williams

August Wilson

BLOOM'S MAJOR NOVELISTS

Jane Austen

The Brontës

Willa Cather

Stephen Crane

Charles Dickens

Fyodor Dostoevsky

William Faulkner

F. Scott Fitzgerald

Thomas Hardy

Nathaniel Hawthorne

Ernest Hemingway

Henry James

James Joyce

D. H. Lawrence

Toni Morrison

John Steinbeck

Stendhal

Leo Tolstoy

Mark Twain

Alice Walker

Edith Wharton

Virginia Woolf

BLOOM'S MAJOR WORLD POETS

Geoffrey Chaucer

Emily Dickinson

John Donne

T. S. Eliot

Robert Frost

Langston Hughes

John Milton

Edgar Allan Poe

Shakespeare's Poems & Sonnets

Alfred, Lord Tennyson

Walt Whitman

William Wordsworth

BLOOM'S MAJOR SHORT STORY WRITERS

William Faulkner

F. Scott Fitzgerald

Ernest Hemingway

O. Henry

James Joyce

Herman Melville

Flannery O'Connor

Edgar Allan Poe

J. D. Salinger

John Steinbeck

Mark Twain

Eudora Welty

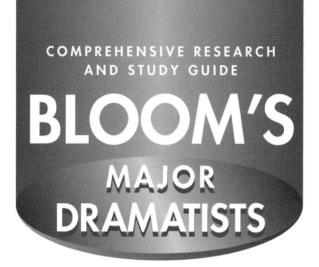

COMPREHENSIVE RESEARCH
AND STUDY GUIDE

BLOOM'S

MAJOR
DRAMATISTS

Oscar
Wilde

EDITED AND WITH AN INTRODUCTION
BY HAROLD BLOOM

First Printing
1 3 5 7 9 8 6 4 2

Library of Congress Cataloging-in-Publication Data
Oscar Wilde / edited and with an introduction by Harold Bloom.
        p. cm. — (Bloom's major dramatists)
    Includes bibliographical references and index.
    ISBN 0-7910-6361-5 (alk. paper)
    1. Wilde, Oscar, 1854–1900—Dramatic works.   I. Bloom, Harold.
II. Series.

PR5827.D7 O83 2001
822'.8—dc21   2001047498

Chelsea House Publishers
1974 Sproul Road, Suite 400
Broomall, PA 19008-0914

The Chelsea House World Wide Web address is
http://www.chelseahouse.com

Series Editor: Matt Uhler

Contributing Editor: Grace Kim

Produced by Publisher's Services, Santa Barbara, California

Contents

User's Guide

This volume is designed to present biographical, critical, and bibliographical information on the author's best-known or most important works. Following Harold Bloom's editor's note and introduction is a detailed biography of the author, discussing major life events and important literary accomplishments. A plot summary of each play follows, tracing significant themes, patterns, and motifs in the work.

A selection of critical extracts, derived from previously published material from leading critics, analyzes aspects of each play. The extracts consist of statements from the author, if available, early reviews of the work, and later evaluations up to the present. A bibliography of the author's writings (including a complete list of all works written, cowritten, edited, and translated), a list of additional books and articles on the author and his or her work, and an index of themes and ideas in the author's writings conclude the volume.

~

Harold Bloom is Sterling Professor of the Humanities at Yale University and Henry W. and Albert A. Berg Professor of English at the New York University Graduate School. He is the author of over 20 books, including *Shelley's Mythmaking* (1959), *The Visionary Company* (1961), *Blake's Apocalypse* (1963), *Yeats* (1970), *A Map of Misreading* (1975), *Kabbalah and Criticism* (1975), *Agon: Toward a Theory of Revisionism* (1982), *The American Religion* (1992), *The Western Canon* (1994), and *Omens of Millennium: The Gnosis of Angels, Dreams, and Resurrection* (1996). *The Anxiety of Influence* (1973) sets forth Professor Bloom's provocative theory of the literary relationships between the great writers and their predecessors. His most recent books include *Shakespeare: The Invention of the Human,* a 1998 National Book Award finalist, and *How to Read and Why,* which was published in 2000.

Professor Bloom earned his Ph.D. from Yale University in 1955 and has served on the Yale faculty since then. He is a 1985 MacArthur Foundation Award recipient, served as the Charles Eliot Norton Professor of Poetry at Harvard University in 1987–88, and has received honorary degrees from the universities of Rome and Bologna. In 1999, Professor Bloom received the prestigious American Academy of Arts and Letters Gold Medal for Criticism.

Currently, Harold Bloom is the editor of numerous Chelsea House volumes of literary criticism, including the series BLOOM'S NOTES, BLOOM'S MAJOR DRAMATISTS, BLOOM'S MAJOR NOVELISTS, MAJOR LITERARY CHARACTERS, MODERN CRITICAL VIEWS, MODERN CRITICAL INTERPRETATIONS, and WOMEN WRITERS OF ENGLISH AND THEIR WORKS.

Editor's Note

My Introduction revisits *The Importance of Being Earnest* in order to pay homage to Lady Bracknell, Wilde's grandest comic creation.

As this volume reprints two dozen critical reviews on all four of Wilde's social comedies, I confine my comments here to just a few of the extracts, choosing those which have had a particular interest for me.

The superb critic of sexual personae, the formidable Camille A. Paglia, argues that Gwendolen and Cecily are of no determinate sexuality, and employ femininity as a mask. Wilde's philosophy of art is invoked by Julia Prewitt Brown to make the strong point that Earnest becomes dated whenever a director fails to take the characters with high seriousness. They must not be played as sophisticated cynics.

Sos Eltis subtly argues that Sir Robert Chiltern embodies Wilde's ironic criticism of nineteenth-century British politics, where selling-out becomes virtuous if it is done at outrageously high prices.

Patricia Flanagan Behrendt studies the sexual implications of the opening scene of *Lady Windermere's Fan,* contrasting the heroine's innocence with Lord Darlington's wicked sophistication. The fan itself is explored by Neil Sammells as a complex representation of rival affections in the play.

A Woman of No Importance is interpreted by Epifanio San Juan Jr. as a clash of feminine change in Hester and of womanly stasis in the anguished Mrs. Arbuthnot. Incest, most dramatic of themes, is invoked by Christopher S. Nassaar, who finds in the play's garden imagery a repressed desire implicit in the relationship between Gerald and Mrs. Arbuthnot.

Introduction

HAROLD BLOOM

I recall writing that, in Lady Augusta Bracknell's rolling periods, Oscar Wilde fused the rhetorical prose styles of Dr. Samuel Johnson and Shakespeare's Sir John Falstaff. "Rise, sir, from this semirecumbent posture. It is most indecorous." competes with: "Human life is everywhere a condition where much is to be endured and little to be enjoyed." And again with: "O thou hast damnable iteration and art indeed able to corrupt a saint. Thou hast done much harm upon me, Hal, God forgive you for it! Before I knew thee, Hal, I knew nothing and now to speak truly am I become little better than one of the wicked." Falstaff is the most elaborate, Johnson the most severe, Bracknell the most outrageous, but all are outrageous enough, and none accepts any demurral.

From her first entrance, Lady Bracknell is on the attack, a dreadnought firing from all turrets:

> Good afternoon, dear Algernon, I hope you are behaving quite well.

She proceeds to disapprove, massively, of the mythical invalid, Bunbury, Algernon's excuse for getting away on country junkets:

> Well, I must say, Algernon, that I think it is high time that Mr. Bunbury made up his mind whether he was going to live or die. This shilly-shallying with the question is absurd.

In some respects, Lady Augusta Bracknell is an ironic prophecy of the Conservative Prime Minister, Dame Margaret Thatcher, iron field marshal of the British victory over the Argentines in the Falklands War. One can see Lady Bracknell in the role, perhaps with Groucho Marx as her adjutant, since heroic farce is her mode. The finest Lady Bracknell I have seen is Dame Edith Evans, in the splendid Anthony Asquith film that features also Michael Redgrave and Margaret Rutherford. Dame Edith played the role as it must be performed, with Wagnerian severity and frowning high seriousness.

Lady Bracknell, a Sublime monster, in some respects is larger than the play, just as the dread Juno is too gigantic a menace even for the *Aeneid.* When I think of Oscar Wilde's work, I always first recall *Earnest,* and then cheer myself up by rolling forth various grand pronouncements of the magnificent Augusta. Wilde said of his greatest play: "It is written by a butterfly for butterflies," which is also very cheering. If Lady Bracknell, in full flight, is a butterfly, then we are listening to an iron butterfly:

> To lose one parent, Mr. Worthing, may be regarded as a misfortune; to lose both looks like carelessness.

> I dislike arguments of any kind. They are always vulgar, and often convincing.

> The General was essentially a man of peace, except in his domestic life.

Lady Bracknell's is the voice of authority, that is to say of social authority, and therefore madness. Her lunacy is founded upon a solipsism so absolute as to be very nearly without rival:

> Come, dear, we have already missed five, if not six, trains. To miss any more might expose us to comment on the platform.

I join my friend Camille Paglia in my passion for this truly gorgeous expression of solipsism. Lady Bracknell's greatness is that she would not comprehend that no one on the platform possibly could know how many trains she had missed, since she cannot conceive of her absence, but only of her overwhelming presence. ❈

Biography of Oscar Wilde

Oscar O'Flahertie Fingal Wills Wilde was born on October 16, 1854, in Dublin, Ireland. He was the younger son of Sir William and Lady Jane Wilde. His mother, a passionate and shrewd woman who evidently formed a great impression upon her second son, was a poet herself, writing under the pseudonym *Speranza*. Lady Wilde held strong aesthetic and political beliefs, and she may very well have served as Wilde's earliest model for his female leads. His father, while renowned as a surgeon, was less credible in his domestic affairs. In Oscar's childhood, the Wilde family became the center of a sensational scandal when a former patient successfully raised a charge of rape against Sir William.

In 1871, Wilde enrolled at Trinity College in Dublin. The years from 1874–1878 were spent at Magdalen College, Oxford, where he received a First Class degree in Classics and the Newdigate Prize for poetry with his submission of *Ravenna*. In London, the young Wilde cheerfully adopted an extravagant and flamboyant life, at times hailing a cab just to cross the street, for the budding dramatist created spectacle as he breathed. Accordingly, Wilde's wardrobe was often central to his constant self-presentation. His clothes were ordered not from a tailor, but from theatre costumiers, and his often outlandish buttonholes of lilies, sunflowers, and green carnations—the underground symbol of aestheticism and homosexuality—became something of a trademark for this outrageous public persona. Yet despite his certain presence in London society, neither Wilde's first play, *Vera, or the Nihilists,* nor his first volume of poetry was particularly well-received. Perhaps as a result of such professional disappointments, Wilde shifted into a more respectable Victorian lifestyle after the early 1880s. He married Constance Lloyd, the daughter of a wealthy Irish barrister in 1884 and had two sons, Cyril and Vyvyan, in the following two years. Through the end of the decade, Wilde edited the fashion journal, *Women's World,* and began publishing criticism and fiction—short stories and fairy tales that he wrote for his sons—in the periodical press. In May 1888, he published *The Happy Prince and Other Tales,* followed by "The Portrait of Mr. W.H." in 1889, and *The Picture of Dorian Gray,* his only novel, in 1890. Yet despite his outward presentation of social and domestic respectability, Oscar maintained a barely covert lifestyle of the brazen dandy. It was during these years that Robert Ross, who eventually published the first collected works of Oscar Wilde after the dramatist's death, was said to have introduced him to the practice of homosexuality.

As many critics and biographers have remarked, Oscar Wilde enjoyed being paradoxical. It is fitting, therefore, that the years recorded as perhaps his most flamboyant and reckless are also recognized as his period of greatest creative productivity. After *The Picture of Dorian Gray,* which received massive critical attention, Wilde went on to write *Salomé* and *Lady Windermere's Fan* in the following year, *A Woman of No Importance* in 1893, and *An Ideal Husband* and *The Importance of Being Earnest,* his dramatic masterpiece, in 1895. *Lady Windermere's Fan, A Woman of No Importance, An Ideal Husband,* and *The Importance of Being Earnest,* referred to collectively as Wilde's social comedies, simultaneously satirized contemporary social mores while sustaining them in apparent high regard. As a dramatist and a member of a notoriously artificial Society, Wilde relished the aspect of performance that imbided the conventions of the day. At the opening night of *Lady Windermere's Fan,* Wilde confused and shocked his audience by making his curtain speech with a cigarette in hand; with his signature green-carnation buttonhole, he complimented them on the success of their performance, implying outrageously that the farce onstage extended to the seated audience.

Critics, often hung between admiration and outrage, were appropriately befuddled by this enigmatic persona, but Wilde seemed ultimately validated when several influential critics of the time, led by William Archer and A. B. Walkley, poured unambiguous praise upon his latest works. Still, Wilde did not enjoy his success for long. By the peak of his production in 1895 with *The Importance of Being Earnest,* Wilde faced a charge of sodomy raised by the Marquess of Queensbury, the father of a young man with whom the dramatist was passionately in love. After months of having his warnings to stay away from his son ignored by the now-famous dramatist, the infuriated Queensbury made public this aspect of Wilde's personal life that became his ruin. Wilde, strongly advised by his mother to defend himself, charged the Marquess with libel, but the evidence found against him proved absolutely damning, and after two trials—

the first ending with a hung jury, and the second with a guilty verdict—Wilde was sentenced to two years of imprisonment and hard labor for his crime of "gross indecency," his affair with the young Lord Alfred Douglas.

During and after his imprisonment, from 1895–1897, Wilde himself concluded that he would never again be the same man that had produced the brilliance of the four social comedies or, perhaps more importantly, the personal energy that had inspired them. In prison, he wrote an extensive letter of confession and admonition addressed to Douglas, which was posthumously published as *De Profundis* Robert Ross in 1905. But even this emotional epistle could not nearly comfort Wilde's great and growing grief at the losses of his life. His beloved mother died of acute bronchitis on February 3, 1896, and while she expressed constant support of her son, whom she recognized as tragically misunderstood, Wilde never recovered from the anguish and shame at his mother's death. By 1897, his wife, Constance made her final separation with Oscar, and he was subsequently refused access to his sons, even after their mother's death in 1898.

After his release from prison, Wilde believed himself unfit for the Society in which he had once thrived, and exiled himself to France, where he adopted the pseudonym "Sebastian Melmoth." Under this name, he published two letters in *The Daily Chronicle* appealing to the public about cruelty to children in British prisons. His final work is a return to poetry, entitled *The Ballad of Reading Gaol,* which he intended to produce for himself a "sacramental" value of intimacy and reconciliation following his experience of imprisonment as a criminal. *The Ballad of Reading Gaol* was a popular success and may have quickened the personal redemption that the dramatist-poet desired. After a trip to Rome in 1900, Wilde fell suddenly and feverishly ill. He died on November 30, 1900, after a deathbed baptism into the Roman Catholic Church in his Paris hotel.

In light of the apparent frivolity of his most famous works, the social comedies, and the sensationalism of his trials, it may often be forgotten that Oscar Wilde, in addition to his writings as a poet and dramatist, also wrote important works of criticism. "The Decay of Lying" (1889) and "The Critic as Artist" (1890) are his best-known essays, collected in the 1891 volume entitled *Intentions.* The four essays in this volume examine art and criticism from a theoretical or philosophical, rather than strictly practical, perspective, to conclude that the spheres of art and ethics are, or should be, entirely distinct and separate. Championing art's autonomy, Oscar Wilde consciously, if not entirely overtly, turned nineteenth-century English aesthetic and social conventions on their heads with a skillful combination of outrage and subtlety that involved his audience into his dramatic addresses, often without their even noticing their crucial role in the play. ❊

Plot Summary of
The Importance of Being Earnest

Algernon's most endearing trait remains his utterly earnest incapacity for remorse, which always assumes that no matter his faults, he will always be granted pardon, and even favor, in the end. It is impossible not to be charmed by such a personage; we suspect that even the chronically disapproving Lady Bracknell does not actually wish her nephew to reform, for his very incorrigibility forms the heart of Algernon's appeal. Still, despite this mischief, Algernon is not a boy or any such diminutive. He is a born actor, performer, entertainer, and he perfectly captures the *modus operandi* of his talent when he remarks to his servant, Lane, in the opening lines of the play: ". . . I don't play accurately—anyone can play accurately—but I play with wonderful expression." Such high style is certainly essential to carry off this character, who sets up a heap of cucumber sandwiches for the visit of his aunt, sternly forbids the good fellow, his friend, Jack/Earnest Worthing, access to the things on grounds of reserving them for Lady Bracknell while in the very act of devouring them himself—and when the lady herself arrives to find only an empty plate where the sandwiches had lately been, her nephew throws up his hands in a perfectly outrageous display of horror and surprise at Lane's deadpan explanation that "there were no cucumbers in the market this morning . . . not even for ready money."

Of course the great joke of this play is that it is of very little importance to anyone that moral earnestness be upheld. Among the four lovers, Jack and Gwendolen, Algernon and Cecily, the two ladies are interested only in the *appearance* of earnestness, as apparently inspired by the word itself, and for both Algernon and Jack, devoted bunburyists, their sole connection with this phantom Earnest-ness lies ironically in their concerted duplicity in having both invoked this great aphrodisiac of names. In fact, the only truly earnest figure in the play is Jack Worthing, the man of exceedingly high virtue that Cecily calls uncle and guardian. Jack Worthing is a fiction of fiction, however, and he exists—somewhat tediously—only in the minds of the few occupants of Cecily's Manor House. Even Lady Bracknell, despite her attention to the social gaze, is rarely in moral earnest—she refuses Jack Gwendolen's hand in marriage due to the unfashionable nature of his origin, and appears quite willing to leave both couples thwarted and unsatisfied in their amorous intentions in favor of catching the afternoon train back to London. In perhaps the most outrageously original lines of the play and perhaps all of Wilde, Lady Bracknell turns her back on the pleading Mr. Worthing, prompting Gwendolen: "Come, dear, we have already missed five, if not six, trains. To miss any more might expose us to comment on the platform." Lady Bracknell, believing that a world of eyes follows her every gesture and look, is absolutely unwilling to allow her imperial image to suffer even imaginary public censure.

Indeed, how many fictional figures are there? There is Mr. Bunbury, a veritable non-being, whom Algernon has created and made terminally ill for his own dallying convenience. Jack Worthing exists, but only in the country; Earnest Worthing plays his in-town counterpart, fondly received by Algernon and Gwendolen and Society at large. A more fictional Earnest Worthing seems also to roam London, for he is Uncle Jack's wicked brother, known only to the cast at Manor House; Jack uses Earnest to excuse himself to town where he relieves himself of the burden of providing a good example for his young charge. Algernon, deciding to honor brother Earnest with a presence at last bunburys himself over to Manor House in order to meet the pretty little niece. She, in turn, brings her visitor in to see his brother only to discover that Jack, having tired of the pretense in light of his recent engagement to Gwendolen, has pronounced wicked brother Earnest dead in Paris. Earnest Worthing, then, pragmatically resurrected by Algernon, takes advantage of his miraculous rebirth to propose to Cecily, who happily accepts, adding hilariously: ". . . it had always been a girlish dream of mine to love some one whose name was Ernest. There is something in that name that seems to inspire absolute confidence. I pity any poor married woman whose husband is not called Ernest."

Who, then, is Earnest? Gwendolen believes herself in love with Earnest Worthing, who is also Jack Worthing. As it plainly appears in her diary, Cecily believes herself to have been engaged to (the idea of) Earnest Worthing for three months. Miraculously, she finds herself actually engaged to a flesh-and-blood Earnest Worthing, who is actually Algernon Moncrieff. In this case, Jack is slightly more Earnest than Algernon is—Algernon has been Earnest only for several hours. But at the end, in a final twist that is more bizarre than even Cecily's accidental prophecy of marriage or Lady Bracknell's absolute self-centeredness, it is Algernon who is Ernest.

In the most farcical of all possible recognition scenes, it is ironically, Miss Prism who becomes the crux of the dramatic turn. Cecily's nervous and over-chaste governess is revealed as Lady Bracknell's former employee, who years ago left her house in disgrace after having misplaced her charge, a baby boy, during one of her errands. The infant, whom she had absurdly mistaken as a bundle of manuscripts she had written, was placed in a hand-bag and left at the Victoria railway station, while the work of fiction was carefully wheeled home in the perambulator. The governess never recovered the boy, and he, handed over to a bewildered but kindly gentleman claiming his bag at the station, grew up right under his aunt's omnipresent gaze as Earnest Worthing, future fiancé of her daughter Gwendolen, and a close fellow of her nephew Algernon. Earnest/Jack Worthing shows a touching generosity of spirit following this revelation. Heroically withholding both judgment and blame, he throws himself at Miss Prism, proclaiming forgiveness and shouting ". . . mother!" even when the prudish governess, recoiling in horror at the affront to her chastity, rebukes: "Mr. Worthing! I am unmarried!" Completely baffled by Miss Prism's refusal to claim him as her long-lost son, Jack can only look to Lady Bracknell for the final clarification. The madam seems not to appreciate the importance of being earnest, for she rather incidentally reveals Jack Worthing's origin as her sister's elder son and Algernon's brother, and cannot remember his given name except that it was his father's Christian name. Thus, another somewhat inevitable delay of dramatic gratification is raised, while Jack rifles through the Army Lists of the period to search for his father's name and discovers that his father was General Ernest John Moncrieff. Overcome with emotion for a moment, he quickly recovers his wit and gloats irreverently: "I always told you, Gwendolen, my name was Ernest, didn't I? Well, it is Ernest after all, I mean it naturally is Ernest. . . . Gwendolen, it is a terrible thing for a man to find out suddenly that all his life he has been speaking nothing but the truth." In these closing lines of the play, we recall, of course, that truth for Ernest Worthing/Moncrieff hinges upon his earnestness, and that his earnestness relies on the importance of being Ernest. Like his newly discovered brother after him, Ernest is a master of triviality, and it is only right that his name should indeed be Ernest, just as it is right that Cecily should have the fictions of her diary recognized as reality. ❀

List of Characters in
The Importance of Being Earnest

John (Jack) Worthing, J.P.: Jack Worthing is a conflicted character. In the country, he is Uncle Jack to his young niece, for whom he has raised himself as a most upstanding example of good breeding and virtue. In town, he is Earnest, a pleasure-loving man of fashion. Earnest, to Cecily, is Uncle Jack's irresponsible younger brother, a fiction that allows Jack to come to town as often as he likes under the pretence of rescuing his brother from yet another scrape. Jack has a most remarkable story of origin, in that he has literally "lost" his parents. As an infant, he was found in a large hand-bag in a railway station coatroom, and raised by the gentleman to whom this hand-bag was mistakenly presented. The farce becomes complete when Jack is revealed to be Algernon's brother.

Algernon Moncrieff: A highly dedicated dandy, who has invented his own term for his amorous activities. "Bunburyism," or alternately, in the active form, "bunburying," refers to Mr. Worthing's trips to the countryside to visit a fictional Mr. Bunbury, an invalid who requires Worthing's frequent sympathy. In truth, Bunbury is merely an excuse and cover designed to allow Jack to visit ladies in the country as he pleases when he tires of London and its Aunt Augustas. Upon learning of Jack Worthing's young charge in the country, Algernon bunburys himself to her house as Jack's "wicked" brother, Earnest, and immediately falls in love with her. Among Algernon's many endearing traits, perhaps his most famous is his restless appetite, especially for cucumber sandwiches.

Lady Bracknell: Algernon's aunt, Lady Augusta Bracknell is a truly formidable woman who lives so fully in the gaze of Society that she is the very embodiment of Society itself. Lady Bracknell is terrifyingly systematic in her relations with people, and takes obedience so for granted that she does not seem to notice when she is disobeyed. The fastest route to her good graces is the possession of a large fortune. All others can and should expect only to face Lady Bracknell's "majestic indignation," her highest and most developed dramatic mode.

Hon. Gwendolen Fairfax: Gwendolen Fairfax is Lady Bracknell's incorrigibly willful daughter. Her cutting frankness and matter-of-fact self-assurance provide a stark contrast to her wildly whimsical adherence to Romance. She accepts Jack Worthing's proposal based on her belief that his name is Earnest, a name that, according to her, "inspires absolute confidence." Gwendolen possesses a great flair for the dramatic, dismissing Lady Bracknell's entrance into the room because she has interrupted the official proposal her daughter was intently directing to her betrothed.

Cecily Cardew: Little Cecily Cardew is Jack Worthing's charge, but she seems hardly to require guidance for she is amazingly self-possessed for her age or any age. Cecily is highly aware of her physical charms, and due to a dearth of real interest in the countryhouse in which she resides, Jack's niece resorts to her own imagination to create for herself a life of drama and intrigue in her diary. At Algernon's immediate infatuation with her and subsequent proposal for marriage, Cecily outrageously replies that that they have already been engaged for three months, as evidenced by careful records in her diary, although in reality, they have only known each other for several hours at most. Cecily is quite as capricious as Gwendolen Fairfax, although the former, benefiting from the puritanical work ethic of her governess, seems to display a sharper intellect than her Society-bred counterpart.

Miss Prism: Cecily's governess, Miss Prism is staunchly devoted to duty and responsibility. She harbors a supposedly covert weakness for Dr. Chasuble, whom she fails to discourage because she does not actually wish to repel him. Miss Prism is finally revealed by Lady Bracknell to be the absent-minded governess who mistakenly left her infant charge, Lady Bracknell's nephew, in a coatroom at a Victoria station twenty-eight years ago.

Rev. Canon Chasuble, D.D.: Once a confirmed celibate, Dr. Chasuble has a change of heart when he decides to ask for Miss Prism's hand in marriage.

Lane: Algernon's perfectly accommodating manservant, he is the master of improvisation, as far as his relations with Algernon's relations are concerned. He possesses a dry wit that only barely conceals a sublime sense of humor, which nevertheless remains strictly concealed throughout the play. ❀

Critical Views on
The Importance of Being Earnest

CHRISTOPHER S. NASSAAR: WILDE'S ORIGINALITY

[Christopher S. Nassaar, Associate Professor of English at the American University of Beirut, is the author of *Into the Demon Universe: A Literary Exploration of Oscar Wilde* (1974) and *Oscar Wilde: The Importance of Being Earnest*, a study guide reprinted annually. He recently completed three further studies on influences on Wilde. In this essay, Nassaar highlights the originality of Oscar Wilde in *The Importance of Being Earnest*.]

The Importance of Being Earnest is essentially a private joke, though the source of its great popularity is Wilde's ability to translate the joke into public terms. By achieving and maintaining a perfect balance between the public and the private, Wilde managed to write one of the most brilliant comic masterpieces of the nineteenth century.

Oscar Wilde's works are often based on earlier ones. *The Picture of Dorian Gray* carefully counterpoints "Lord Arthur Savile's Crime" while providing *Lady Windermere's Fan* with its basic theme. *A Woman of No Importance* is thematically a repetition of *Salome,* while its wit is borrowed largely from *Dorian Gray. An Ideal Husband* harks back to the fairy tales in theme. *The Importance of Being Earnest* is the least self-contained of Wilde's works, for it is rooted not in one but in practically all of them. It is, moreover, an entirely original play. Wilde was later to write, in *De Profundis:* "I took the drama, the most objective form known to art, and I made it as personal a mode of expression as the lyric or the sonnet, at the same time that I widened its range and enriched its characterization."

If *Earnest* has exasperated the critics, it is because of this complete originality. Without doubt, it widened the range of the drama. Drama had been used subjectively before, by the Romantics, but Wilde here carried it to the outer limits of subjectivity and thus provided us with probably the most personal, private play in existence—a play that is basically a self-parody. Forever a lover of paradox, he took the most objective form known to literature and treated it entirely subjectively. The opening lines suggest what sort of a drama this is going to be:

> ALGERNON. Did you hear what I was playing, Lane?
> LANE. I didn't think it polite to listen, sir.
> ALGERNON. I'm sorry for that, for your sake. I don't play accurately—any one can play accurately—but I play with wonderful expression. As far as the piano is concerned, sentiment is my forte.

Algy's piano-playing is an art, but he aims through it purely to express a mood. Lane regards this art as private and discreetly turns a deaf ear, but had he listened he would have had an enjoyable experience.

Like Algy's piano-playing, *The Importance of Being Earnest* aims purely at creating a mood, and it succeeds so brilliantly that audiences have been applauding since 1895. It is the object of this analysis to show that the play also has a private meaning that is wholly consistent with its humorous trivial mood. The meaning—not necessary to an enjoyment of *Earnest*—reinforces the mood and adds an extra comic dimension to the play. To see the play's dialogue as constituting an anti-Victorian barrage—as Eric Bentley does—or to condemn it as depraved—as Mary McCarthy does—is really to be untrue to its tone and unappreciative of its originality. Even Richard Ellmann misses the mark—though not by much—when he sees the play's theme as being sin and crime, treated indifferently and rendered harmless. ⟨. . .⟩

Not all the play's wit is harmless, though. Some of it has the potential to corrupt too, and this is especially true of Algy's comments about marriage. "Divorces are made in Heaven," Algy remarks, then soon afterward observes that "in married life three is company and two is none." In the mouth of Wotton, such comments would have had a disastrous effect on Dorian. In *Earnest*, however, the comments are amusing but harmless. They have no effect on Jack, to whom they are addressed, or on Algy, who utters them. Both pursue the goal of marriage in the play and end up happily married. At one point, Algy repeats a famous epigram of Wotton's:

> ALGERNON. All women become like their mothers. That is their tragedy. No man does. That's his.

JACK. Is that clever?

ALGERNON. It is perfectly phrased! and quite as true as any observation in civilized life should be.

In this brief exchange, Wilde concisely sums up his attitude toward
Wotton in *The Importance of Being Earnest*. Wotton's corrupt,
immoral epigrams are now seen as toothless. Wit exists because it is
perfectly phrased, and for no other reason. The play is full of witty
comments whose only purpose is to be perfectly phrased and therefore highly amusing—wit for wit's sake, so to speak.

> —Christopher S. Nassaar, *Into the Demon Universe: A Literary Explo-
> ration of Oscar Wilde* (New Haven, Conn.: Yale University Press,
> 1974): pp. 130–132, 138.

JOEL FINEMAN: THE SIGNIFICANCE OF LITERATURE IN *THE IMPORTANCE OF BEING EARNEST*

[Joel Fineman taught at the University of California,
Berkeley, specializing in 16th- and 17th-century English Literature. He is the author of *Shakespeare's Perjured Eye: The
Invention of Poetic Subjectivity in the Sonnets* (1986). In this
essay, Fineman explicates Jack-Ernest Worthing's character
as the self's relation to writing.]

> Man, poor, awkward, reliable, necessary man belongs to a
> sex that has been rational for millions and millions of
> years. He can't help himself. It is in his race. The History
> of Women is very different. We have always been pic-
> turesque protests against the mere existence of common
> sense. We saw its dangers from the first.
> —*A Woman of No Importance*

What I am outlining here summarizes portions of a longer essay I
have been writing on Oscar Wilde's *The Importance of Being Earnest*.
For the most part, I will forego discussion of the play and focus on
the way in which Wilde's farce precisely figures the problem of "The
Self in Writing." You will perhaps recall that Jack-Ernest, the hero of

the play, discovers the unity of his duplicity when he learns that as an infant he was quite literally exchanged for writing in the cloakroom of Victoria Station, his absent-minded governess having substituted for his person the manuscript of a three-volume novel which is described as being "of more than usually repulsive sentimentality." As a result, because Jack-Ernest is in this way so uniquely and definitively committed to literature, with literature thus registered as his alter-ego, he is one of those few selves or subjects whose very existence, as it is given to us, is specifically literary, an ego-ideal of literature, as it were, whose form is so intimately immanent in his content as to collapse the distinction between a name and that which it bespeaks, and whose temporal destiny is so harmoniously organic a whole as to make it a matter of natural fact that his end be in his beginning—for Ernest is indeed, as Lady Bracknell puts it, paraphrasing traditional definitions of allegory, one whose origins are in a terminus.

Yet if Jack-Ernest is thus an ideal image of the relation of the self to writing, he is nevertheless himself a piece of literature, and therefore but a literary representation of the self's relation to literature, a fiction, therefore, if not necessarily a farce, and for this reason not to be trusted. This is the difficulty, I take it, that our forum has been established to address, recognizing that while the self and writing are surely implicated each in the other, perhaps even reciprocally constitutive each *of* the other, they are so in a way that at the same time undermines the integrity and the stability of both. This we can see even in the delicate phrasing of our forum's title, where the vagueness of the preposition, the problematic and diffusive metaphoricity of its innocuous "in"—"The Self *in* Writing"—testifies to the fact that the Self *and* Writing, as literal categories with their own propriety, can only be linked together in a figural discourse, which, even as it is spoken, calls the specificity and the literality of its terms into question. Strictly speaking, of course, "The Self in Writing" is an impossible locution, for in writing we do not find the self but, at best, only its representation, and it is only because *in* literature, in a literary mode, we characteristically, if illegitimately, rush to collate a word both with its sense and with its referent that we are, even momentarily, tempted to forget or to suspend the originary and intrinsic difference between, on the one hand, the self who reads, and, on the other, the literary revision of that self who is read.

This is to insist upon the fact that the self's relation to literature is not itself a literary relation, and that only a sentimental and literary reading will obsessively identify a thing with its word, a signified with its signifier, or the self with its literary image. This is also to avoid simplistic dialectical accounts of the act of reading—either identificatory or implicative—whose mechanical symmetries programmatically reduce the self to its idealization: the so-called "ideal reader" of whom we hear a great deal of late. Instead, this is to recognize that if we are to speak of the relation of the self to the writing in which it finds itself written, or, stylizing this familiar topos, if we are to speak of the relation of the self to the language in which it finds itself bespoken, then we must do so in terms of a critical discourse that registers the disjunction and the discrepancy between being and meaning, thing and word, and which therefore locates the self who is committed to language in its experience of the slippage between its immediate presence to itself and its mediated representation of itself in a symbolic system. Moreover, since Being, to be thought, must be thought as Meaning, even this self-presence of the self to itself will emerge only in retrospect as less, with the self discovering itself in its own meaningful aftermath, just as Being can only be spoken in its own effacement, as Heidegger—not Derrida—has taught us.

As is well known, it is thanks to the patient, painstaking, and rigorous labors of the tradition of psychoanalysis—a tradition that begins with Freud and which probably concludes with Lacan—that we possess a theoretical vocabulary sufficiently supple to capture this subject born in the split between self-presence and the representation of self. The insights of this tradition, however perfunctorily and schematically I refer to them here, are what enable us to situate the self of "The Self in Writing" in the metaphorical *in* whose very figurality is what allows us to articulate the problem in the first place, which is to say, in the same displacing place that Wilde—whose play will thematize this very problem of the place of the subject—places *Being,* midway between the import of *Importance* and a specifically literary pun on *Earnest*—the importance of *being Earnest*—as though the indeterminacy of meaning in turn determined *Being* as its own rueful double entendre.

—Joel Fineman, "The Significance of Literature: *The Importance of Being Earnest," October* 15 (Winter 1980).

[Katharine Worth is Professor of English Literature at Royal Holloway College and Emeritus Professor of Drama at King's College, London. Her books include *Samuel Beckett's Theatre: Life Journeys, The Irish Drama of Europe from Yeats to Beckett, Maeterlinck's Plays in Performance,* and *Oscar Wilde.* She has also edited *Beckett the Shape Changer: A Symposium.* In this selection, Worth highlights Wilde's use of musical devices in language, and traces his dramatic legacy in the numerous revisions of his plays.]

With *The Importance of Being Earnest* Wilde anticipated a major development in the twentieth century, the use of farce to make fundamentally serious (not earnest!) explorations into the realm of the irrational. The play has been immensely influential, serving as model for writers as diverse as T. S. Eliot, who gave a religious turn to the foundling motif in *The Confidential Clerk* (1953), and Charles Wood, in his bleakly funny play about the Second World War, *Dingo* (1969), which has British soldiers performing *The Importance of Being Earnest* in a German prison camp. Wilde's devotees, Joe Orton and Tom Stoppard, have paid especially full tribute to his genius. Orton, whose life has features in common with Wilde's (homosexuality, traumatic experience of prison), said that his aim was to write a play as good as *The Importance of Being Earnest.* He came very near to doing this in *What the Butler Saw* (1969), a more manic version, in the vulgar postcard, sexy style proclaimed by its title, of Wilde's farce of identity: characters split into two, commandeer each other's identities, discover that they really are what they thought they were only pretending to be, in a way which continually acknowledges the Wildean source. While by "borrowing" characters and whole episodes from *The Importance of Being Earnest* for his *Travesties,* Tom Stoppard demonstrates his belief that the play has entered the collective unconscious in the same way as the other masterpiece he uses in his own drama, *Hamlet.* Only if the play does indeed have that status, could the jokes of *Travesties* work to the full and the ruling ideas come over. *Travesties* is from first to last a piece of Wildean play on the relation between life and art in which everyone is juggling roles; Carr, who is never really in the play he thinks he is in, the Dadaist proclaiming "Pleasure, pleasure," the girls who enact the tea-party scene line for line as if they did not know they were playing it, the ideal butler who turns out to be a secret Leninist and James Joyce playing an Irish comedian version of the real James Joyce who played in *The Importance of Being Earnest* in Zurich in 1917.

Wilde would surely have been amused by all this tongue-in-the-cheek play with his play. Still less can one doubt that he would have approved W. H. Auden's comment that *The Importance of Being Earnest* was "the only pure verbal opera in English." In none of his plays, not even *Salomé,* is the musical treatment more pronounced. Verbal music is heightened by a host of musical devices and allusions; as in opera the curtain rises to the sound of music (Algernon's piano playing); Lady Bracknell contributes a Wagnerian peal and pays idiosyncratic tribute to the power of music by banning French songs from Algernon's concert programme; the spoken word moves irresistibly nearer the condition of music till the lovers are keeping the beat dictated by Gwendolen's uplifted forefinger, practically singing and dancing. Perhaps it is not surprising that actors have had difficulty in capturing this intricate stylisation. Modern actors may not make the same mistake as their Victorian predecessors:—at least they know to keep a straight face—and no doubt many modern productions have come nearer to Wilde's conception than the first ones did. But they may also have become more stereotyped. Some famous performances have come to be thought of as definitive: Edith Evans's magnificently sonorous "A hand-bag," Margaret Rutherford's piquantly obsessed Miss Prism, have established themselves rightly as high peaks in comic acting. These admired styles seem also to have fixed the pattern from which actors find it hard to move away. As Irving Wardle said of the 1982 National Theatre production, everyone was waiting to see how Judi Dench would handle the classic handbag line. Her low-key treatment (she concentrated on tearing up her notes on Jack's eligibility as a suitor) was in tune with a new conception of the role which preserved the veneer but allowed more of the human being to peep out from behind it.

In the post-Orton world we might hope for performances of *The Importance of Being Earnest* that would take yet another line and realize the "heartlessness" so troublesome to Shaw in bold, modern terms, bringing out the subversive and surreal elements. Such a production would have to end on a different note however, from the anarchic stupefaction of *What the Butler Saw.* Wilde does indeed, like Orton, show the world as tending to cruelty and heartlessness, life as an absurd performance, personality as a fluid thing, endlessly forming and reforming itself with the aid of masks (an emphasis on impermanence that alarmed even Yeats, the master of masks). But Wilde's optimistic, benevolent nature required a more harmonious ending for his farce than anything Orton, or perhaps any modern existentialist, would be likely to envisage. *The Importance of Being Earnest* ends with all the dissonances resolved and harmony achieved. It can only happen in Utopia, which means "nowhere"— but as Wilde said, "A map of the world that does not include Utopia is not worth even glancing at, for it leaves out the one country at which Humanity is always landing."

> —Katharine Worth, *Oscar Wilde* (New York: Grove Press, 1983): pp. 137–138

CAMILLE A. PAGLIA: OSCAR WILDE AND THE ENGLISH EPICENE

[Camille A. Paglia taught at Bennington College from 1972–1979 and at the Philadelphia University of the Arts since 1987, where she became Professor of Humanities in 1991. She is the author of *Sexual Personae: Art and Decadence from Nefertiti to Emily Dickinson; The Birds; Sex, Art, and American Culture: Essays;* and *Vamps and Tramps: New Essays.* In this essay, Paglia discusses Wilde's highly mannered presentation of sexuality and youth in his London stage society.]

In *The Importance of Being Earnest* the courtship of youth and maiden, at the traditional heart of comedy, loses its emotional color in the Wildean transformation of content into form, of soul into surface. Jack Worthing and Algernon Moncrieff, idle gentlemen-about-town, and Gwendolen Fairfax and Cecily Cardew, the well-bred objects of their affections, are all Androgynes of Manners. They have no sex because they have no real sexual feelings. The interactions of the play are governed by the formalities of social life, which emerge with dancelike ritualism. The key phrase of the English fin de siècle was Lionel Johnson's axiom, "Life must be a ritual." In *The Picture of Dorian Gray* Wilde says: "The canons of good society are, or should be, the same as the canons of art. Form is absolutely essential to it. It should have the dignity of a ceremony, as well as its unreality." In *The Importance of Being Earnest* the ceremony of social form is stronger than gender, shaping the personae to its public purpose and turning the internal world into the external. ⟨. . .⟩

Gwendolen is the first of the women to enact a drama of form. Soliciting Jack to propose to her, she announces in advance that she will accept him but still insists that her bewildered suitor perform the traditional ritual, on his knees. Gwendolen's thoughts never stray from the world of appearances. At the climax of their romantic interlude, she says to Jack, "I hope you will always look at me just like that, especially when there are other people present." This voyeuristic series of observers is a psychosexual topos of Decadent Late Romanticism, first occurring in 1835 in Gautier's *Mademoiselle de Maupin.* Gwendolen imagines Jack looking at her while she looks at others looking at *them.* As a worshipper of form, Gwendolen craves not emotion but display, the theater of social life.

Gwendolen's self-observing detachment is exhibited by Cecily in precisely the same situation. When Algernon ardently declares his love for her, Cecily replies, "If you will allow me, I will copy your remarks into my diary." Emotion is immediately dispatched into a self-reflexive Mannerist torsion. Going to her writing table, Cecily exhorts her suitor to continue his protestations: "I delight in taking down from dictation." Intimacy is swelled into oratory, and poor Algernon is like Alice grown suddenly too big for the White Rabbit's house. Despite their impending marriage, Cecily declares it quite out of the question for Algernon to see her diary. Nevertheless, it is "meant for publication": "When it appears in volume form I hope you will order a copy." The Sibylline archivist, with professional impartiality, grants no special privileges to her sources of data.

Never for a moment in the play are Gwendolen and Cecily persuasively "female." They are creatures of indeterminate sex who take up the mask of femininity to play a new and provocative role. The dandified Algernon and Jack are simply supporting actors whom the women boldly stage manage. Gwendolen and Cecily are adepts of a dramaturgical alchemy: they are Cerberuses on constant guard to defend the play against encroachment by the internal, which they magically transform into the external. *The Importance of Being Earnest* is one long process of crystallization of the immaterial into the material, of emotion into self-conscious personae. In Shakespeare's volatile Rosalind and Cleopatra, automanipulation of personae arises from a Renaissance abundance of emotion, which flows into a multiplicity of psychodramatic forms. But Wilde's Gwendolen and Cecily inhabit a far more stringently demarcated world, the salon of the Androgyne of Manners, and their personae are radically despiritualized, efflorescences not of psyche but of couture.

—Camille A. Paglia, "Oscar Wilde and the English Epicene," Raritan: A Quarterly Review 4, no. 3 (Winter 1985): pp. 85–109.

☙

KERRY POWELL: ALGERNON'S OTHER BROTHERS

[Kerry Powell is the author of *Women and Victorian Theatre* (1997) and *Oscar Wilde and the Theatre of the 1890s* (1990). In this excerpt, Powell locates *The Importance of Being Earnest* within the historical and dramatic context of Wilde's contemporaries.]

Wilde could not have written *The Importance of Being Earnest* without a thorough, practical knowledge of what was being done in the lowly theatrical genre of farce in the 1890s. He would have had, without the example of his obscure forerunners, little or nothing to say. Yet *Earnest* has survived, while nearly all the others perished utterly after their moment in the footlights. What distinguished Wilde's play—besides its publication as a book—was an undercurrent of seriousness which was mostly absent among other farces of the day.

Nothing could be more mistaken than the popular and traditional view of Wilde's play as a wisp of fantasy, void of significance and unconnected even to reality. As Richard Ellmann has pointed out, *Earnest* resembles Wilde's earlier work in leading toward a ceremonial unmasking, its characters, like their creator, craving to show what they are. In addition to serving as a staging ground for identity, the play's concern with appearances (Algy "has nothing but he looks everything") may be, in part, Wilde's comment on a society of spectacle in which "all that mattered was the authority of the participants' poses and the glitter of their props." Wilde's subjects, as Eric Bentley observes, are death, money, marriage, sociology, economics, and the class system, and his "flippancies repeated, developed, and, so to say, elaborated almost into a system amount of something in the end—and thereby cease to be flippant." Katharine Worth finds in *Earnest* Wilde's "supreme demolition of late nineteenth-century social and moral attitudes, the triumphal conclusion to his career as revolutionary moralist." It is highly ironic that Wilde achieved such effects in *Earnest* by using the mechanisms he had employed in the society dramas, with their almost fatal hesitations between sentimental morality and the dandy's world of pure form. Here again are women with a past, "ideal" yet guilty males, motifs of hidden parentage and mistaken identity, and the pivotal plot-object (handbag rather than fan). These similarities illustrate the close relation of farce and melodrama, as Worth has shown, but also the difference between the two forms. Once out of melodrama, Wilde could dissolve in the dandy's laughter the notions of sin and guilt that were so potent, and disruptive, in his previous works. ⟨. . .⟩

If Wilde supplied himself with characters, situations, and speeches from the ample warehouse of *fin-de-siècle* farce, he also instilled his play with qualities which distinguish it from other comedies of the kind. *The Importance of Being Earnest* is characterized, above all, by an intellectual coherence and thematic solidity which are notably absent in its precursors. It is, as the playwright subtitled it, "A Trivial Comedy for Serious People." ⟨. . .⟩

In 1895, the year *Earnest* was staged, Henry Arthur Jones brought out *The Renascence of the English Drama,* admonishing playwrights to provide their audiences with an "interpretation of life" rather than merely "funny or sensational theatrical things." Wilde's play satisfies this standard, although not in the way intended by Jones, who wished theatres to become the cathedrals of a secular age. Neither Jones himself, imbued with ideas of Arnoldian culture, nor the farcical dramatists who preceded Wilde would have permitted their heroes to assert, as Jack Worthing does, that "a high moral tone can hardly be said to conduce very much to either one's health or one's happiness." But it is language of this sort which makes *The Importance of Being Earnest* more than merely "funny." All through its dialogue runs a current of generalization which bestows upon the characters and their behavior a significance beyond themselves.

> —Kerry Powell, *Oscar Wilde and the Theatre of the 1890s* (Cambridge, England: Cambridge University Press, 1990): pp. 124–139.

⚘

JULIA PREWITT BROWN: WILDE'S PHILOSOPHY OF ART

[Julia Prewitt Brown is Professor of English at Boston University, specializing in 19th-Century British literature. She is author of *Cosmopolitan Criticism: Oscar Wilde's Philosophy of Art* (1997) and "Jane Austen's Novels: Social Change and Literary Form" (1979). In this selection, Professor Brown emphasizes Wilde's unique blend of seriousness and triviality in his rituals of language and naming in *The Importance of Being Earnest.*]

In this vibrating linguistic universe, "The only really safe name is Ernest," says a character, wisely concerned with safety. In order to participate in the society or its institutions, such as marriage, some claim to a consistent identity must be made so that we may recognize one another, literally by *name.* Knowing this (in a play in which all of the characters are so innocently knowing), Jack and Algernon seek to establish themselves in the hearts and minds of the women characters by means of baptism, the naming ritual. It would seem that in the world of play "there is no event or thing . . . that does not in some way partake of language. . . . We cannot imagine a total absence of language in anything." Wilde playfully anticipates Benjamin's philosophy of language (in "The Critic as Artist" he had written that language is "the parent, and not the child of thought"), although keeping it within a predictable set of 'realistic' human concerns.

Not that *The Importance of Being Earnest* is without magic. A character who never existed is brought back to life when someone claims his name; characters come up with pasts for one another by pointing to a diary, register, and handbag. But all of this is understood by an audience whose response takes the form of rational amusement, not simply over the supposed ubiquitousness of language, but over the characters' earnest relation to it. In order for the play to amuse, the absolute earnestness of the characters' prattle must be taken for granted. For although each character is an assemblage of words, each possesses an *intention:* the intention to marry. Wilde returns playfully to the biological origins of the comic genre in this most cerebral of plays. In the Anthony Asquith film version of the play, for example, Michael Redgrave plays Jack as someone wholly earnest and in love, who can barely hold a teacup without dropping it when in the presence of his beloved. Irony, wit, cynicism are qualities strangely external to the characters in this performance, who are wholly unconscious of what they are saying. When Cecily is about to meet the man she thinks is her scapegrace cousin, she says: "I have never met any really wicked person before. I feel rather frightened. I am so afraid he will look just like everyone else." And after she meets him she says indignantly: "I hope you have not been leading a double life, pretending to be wicked and being really good all the time. That would be hypocrisy." The humor is not simply in what she is saying but in her absolute earnestness toward the man with whom she has already fallen in love. Our emotions, as an audience, are thus engaged not by our sense of the characters' innocence but by their charm. By conventional standards, they are all, every one of them, corrupt. But Wilde's aim is to suggest that not all *standards* are serious.

The only thing that could date *The Importance of Being Earnest,* then, would be if directors ceased to take the characters seriously and misdirected the actors to perform with knowing wit and cynicism. This happens from time to time in revivals that fail because of their insipidity. The humor of the play depends upon the characters' absolutely terrifying dependence on the power of language and naming. As in Charlie Chaplin's performances, we must fear for the comic figure in order to be amused by him, and to fear for him we must trust his intentions. The tension in this sort of comedy, which resembles that accompanying the acrobatic paradoxes of "The Decay of Lying," is something that we must bear, as we watch, for example, Chaplin roller-skate on the edge of a precipice. In the *Laws,* Plato said that we must learn to bear pleasure as well as pain, and those who dislike *The Importance of Being Earnest* (like George Bernard Shaw and Mary McCarthy, who found it to be cold-hearted) are perhaps unprepared to do this. It was Wilde's contention that in his century people as a rule were far more prepared to bear pain than pleasure, and found the former far easier to do. Each generation has its revival of *The Importance of Being Earnest* to remind us of this task. Because of its perpetual challenge, the play is still ahead of its time. Wilde knew he was playing with fire when he wrote it: "How I used to toy with that tiger Life!" he wrote to Reginald Turner, possibly alluding to the homosexual subtext of the action: the secret life of "bunburying." Having passed through the purifying fires of the earlier plays in which a Christian aesthetic of pain is exorcised, Wilde, who literally had to bear his pleasures, understood that pleasure is as realizable as pain. To bear pleasure—that is, to suffer it as well as to give it birth—is what the play is about, a burden that has everything to do with language. For Algernon and Jack do not move forward in time toward death, but backward in time toward their own christening, to the paradisiac moment of naming. After this creative moment, after the fall into language, all else becomes empty "prattle," in the profound sense in which Kierkegaard uses the word. That *The Importance of Being Earnest* is composed of such prattle is what disturbed Mary McCarthy, who compared it to the suffocating world of Jean-Paul Sartre's *No Exit*. Yet within that idle world of prattle Algernon and Jack work surprisingly hard toward freeing themselves of it by returning to the original word, which, ironically enough, is *earnest* (or Ernest).

The abrupt conclusion of the action, in which the pun on "being Ernest" is loudly proclaimed and the play seems to disappear into the sky like a balloon whose string has been cut, intensifies our feeling that the play's language is a labyrinth in which the characters are forever doomed to wander and play, utterly separate from the circumstantial world in which we ourselves live. This lightness is an essential element in Wilde's theory of art in general; and, as Adorno suggests, it holds for art as a whole, even works preoccupied with the horrors of reality: "Even in Beckett's plays the curtain rises the way it rises on the room with the Christmas presents." But *The Importance of Being Earnest* is unique—"a genre in itself," as critics have recognized—in its delight in the fact of its own existence, that it is art at all. It was in the period of its composition that Wilde's utopianism in fact peaked. On holiday in Algiers shortly before the first trial, he had remarked to Gide, "The sun is jealous of art."

—Julia Prewitt Brown, *Cosmopolitan Criticism: Oscar Wilde's Philosophy of Art* (Charlottesville: University of Virginia Press, 1997): pp. 89–91.

Plot Summary of
An Ideal Husband

One would regret very much to have *An Ideal Husband* performed without the audience being acquainted with the written version of the play. A dramatic performance cannot represent the priceless descriptions of each character given in the stage directions, which introduce each person by comparing him or her to the appropriate work of art he or she resembles. Aside from the purely entertaining function of this exercise, Wilde employs such explicit comparisons to imply that this is a drama in which the characters regard each other as 'pure' representations, idealizations of both fiction and reality such that whole relationships sustain themselves by a careful preservation of the ideal.

Of the major characters, Lord Goring is the only one who is not compared to an artistic form. Wilde describes Lady Chiltern as a Greek beauty, Sir Robert Chiltern as a potential Vandyck portrait, Miss Mabel as a Tanagra statuette, and Mrs. Cheveley as "a work of art, on the whole, but showing the influence of too many schools."

As in *Lady Windermere's Fan* and *A Woman of No Importance*, the action of *An Ideal Husband* is completed within twenty-four hours. Tension rises quite early in the play, when Lady Chiltern, greeting guests at her party, recognizes her old schoolmate, who now calls herself Mrs. Cheveley. By the end of the first act, Lady Chiltern explains her cold reception of her guest to her husband, revealing that Mrs. Cheveley, even as a girl, was dishonest and thieving. Still, Gertrude's revelation cannot help her husband, who has already become hopelessly ensnared by Mrs. Cheveley, who possesses a very damning piece of evidence against the apparently blameless Sir Robert and appears determined to use this information to her advantage. In his youth, the endlessly ambitious Robert gained his fortune by selling to one Baron Arnheim, a Stock Exchange specu-lator, a Cabinet secret regarding the purchase of the Suez Canal. The deal made both men quite wealthy—the Baron because he bought shares in the Canal, knowing three days before anyone else the Gov-ernment's acquisition of it, and Chiltern, because the Baron com-pensated the young man handsomely for the tip. Mrs. Cheveley, businesslike from the start, requires that Sir Robert use his position to support the Argentine Canal Company, in which she and her friends have heavily—but mistakenly—invested. In return, she will hand over the disastrous letter that Chiltern had written to the Baron regarding their illicit transaction.

Mrs. Cheveley is unscrupulous, faithless, perhaps even evil, but her observation of society is flawless. Her threat to Sir Robert rests precisely on the cutting accuracy of her perception, the gatherings of which she lays maddeningly before him: "Remember to what a point your Puritanism in England has brought you. In old days nobody pretended to be a bit better than his neighbours. In fact, to be a bit better than one's neighbour was considered excessively vulgar and middle-class. Nowadays, with our modern mania for morality, every one has to pose as a paragon of purity, incorruptibility, and all the other seven deadly virtues—" Pointing out that the London newspapers would greedily print his scandal and watch his ruin the minute she let the letter into the proper hands, Mrs. Cheveley gives Sir Robert no possible escape, and he agrees to her base proposal. However, Chiltern's troubles more than multiply when Gertrude, informed of Mrs. Cheveley's request of her husband by the woman herself, insists that he write her immediately and deny his agreement. Wilde certainly shows Sir Robert little gentleness in his distress, for in the closing lines of Act One, Lady Chiltern, despite her good intentions, unwittingly speaks words that seem designed to invoke a torture most particularly suited to her husband's predicament. Responding to Robert's desperate pleas that she love him always, she placidly returns that she will always love him because he "will always be worthy of love," not realizing that this is exactly what he fears, that she will find him no longer 'worthy' of love if his secret is revealed. Robert feels that he must do whatever is necessary to remain worthy, but whether this is by protecting his secret or by following her wishes in defaming Mrs. Cheveley's proposal, he cannot decide.

When Sir Robert turns to his closest friend for advice, Lord Goring is sympathetic but amazed that Robert will not tell Gertrude of his situation. "Is Lady Chiltern as perfect as all that?" he asks, obviously amused even through his worry. Lord Goring, despite his efforts to appear anything but thoughtful, is an authentic philosopher disguised by impeccable tailoring. His counsel to his tormented friend contains a perfect blend of the dandy and the sage: "Everything is dangerous, my dear fellow. If it wasn't so, life wouldn't be worth living . . . Well, I am bound to say that I think you should have told her years ago."

Robert Chiltern is indeed in danger, but it is important to note that his distress is, as Mrs. Cheveley implies, strictly circumstantial. He does not repent of having compromised himself no more than he regrets his fortune and social position, which were born of that moral compromise. In their first meeting, Robert, utterly bewildered by the blow that he has just received from Mrs. Cheveley, cries out: "My God! what brought you into my life?" She replies in a word: "Circumstances." The truth of this provides an uncomfortable connection between two characters, one whom we regard as the protagonist and the other the obvious antagonist. Both Robert Chiltern and Mrs. Cheveley, at moments of crucial consequence, form their behavior according to circumstance. Sir Robert, having made himself a prominent political figure with the capital from his reprehensible dealings with the Baron, upheld from that point forth a character of high morality and principle, a stance that brought him public respect throughout his career. A man who looks his closest friend in the eyes and claims the injustice of the consequences of his own sins, who finds Machiavelian justification in his own reckless ambition for power and wealth has much in common with his antagonist, who, likewise, vindicates herself from guilt by her belief that she merely acts on her own behalf as everyone does, and not by any malice at all.

By the end of the second act, Mrs. Cheveley herself reveals Robert's secret to his wife, and here, it is difficult to believe that there is no malice in her conscious destruction of domestic trust between the Chilterns. Gertrude, thrown into a despair even deeper than that of her husband, writes Lord Goring a note expressing her intention to come to him for help. But here the stage is set for crucial misunderstandings: Lord Goring, expecting Lady Chiltern, instructs his servant that he is to be home to no one that evening except for a lady soon to arrive. Phipps, met at the door by Mrs. Cheveley, assumes that she is the lady about whom his master made mention, and ushers her into a room to await Lord Goring, who has become waylaid by a surprise visit from his father. Another unexpected visitor, this time Sir Robert appears at the door, and Lord Goring, believing that Lady Chiltern waits within earshot in the next room, leads Robert to conversation which he hopes will help make his wife understand his trouble. When Mrs. Cheveley, not Lady Chiltern, steps out from behind the door, both men are completely startled, and Sir Robert, believing that Arthur Goring has betrayed him, leaves his house in anger. Still, the misfortunes of this night have yet to end for Lord Goring, who scores a temporary victory when he successfully accuses, and subsequently counter-blackmails, Mrs. Cheveley as the thief of a valuable diamond-and-ruby bracelet that he had given to his cousin ten years ago. In return for not handing her over to the police, Lord Goring acquires the wretched letter, which he burns. But that is not the last of unfortunate correspondences—Mrs. Cheveley, snatching up the note that Lady Chiltern, in her distress, had written to Lord Goring, exits with the last word, by saying that she will send the letter, regrettably misinterpretable, to Robert Chiltern as a love-letter from his wife to his closest friend.

All's well that ends well—Mrs. Cheveley, carelessly does not include an explanation of her interpretation of Lady Chiltern's letter in the envelope to Sir Robert, and when he receives it—without the original envelope from Mrs. Cheveley—assumes that the note is for him, as it is in his wife's hand, and no more is thought of either spouse's potential domestic dangers. Although politically out of danger as well, Sir Robert intends to decline the fulfillment of his ambition, an appointment to the Cabinet, for the sake of Gertrude's approval. Once again, it is Lord Goring who is the ultimate voice of reason for the Chilterns, and he convinces Lady Chiltern that she must require such a vast and empty sacrifice from her husband. All transactions and sacrifices resolved, the curtain falls on Gertrude and Robert, who have, despite their recent transformations, raised yet another ideal of love for one another, and Arthur and his newly betrothed Mabel, whose charm still struggles to escape the ideal into reality: "An ideal husband! Oh, I don't think I should like that. It sounds like something in the next world. . . . He can be what he chooses. All I want is to be . . . to be . . . oh! a real wife to him." ❀

List of Characters in
An Ideal Husband

The Earl of Caversham, K.G.: Lord Caversham is described as "a fine Whig type" who quite vocally disapproves of his dandy son, Lord Goring. Age seventy, the Earl has developed a well-groomed irritation for Society. Still, it is to his shame that Lord Caversham does not know his son very well, for he joins Society in idealizing Robert Chiltern, never realizing his own son's role in preserving that idealization.

Viscount Goring: Lord Goring, among Wilde's dandies, is an extremely likeable character whose actual dandyism remains restricted to his dress and his speech for he is a very sincere man at heart. He single-handedly saves the Chiltern marriage and Sir Robert's career, because he alone really understands both Robert and Gertrude Chiltern. Lord Goring is perfectly good-natured and strikingly frank in his observation of the world. While he tells his father that he lives entirely for pleasure, he also repeatedly rejects his father's claim that he is heartless by a literally expressed, "I hope not, father."

Sir Robert Chiltern, Bart.: Under-Secretary for Foreign Affairs. Sir Robert is the most esteemed politician and "ideal husband" of England. Rightly so, for his sound scruples and domestic perfection are as well-known as his success. Mrs. Cheveley holds the only evidence of his imperfection, the illicit origin of his wealth, which she threatens to make public unless he uses his political power to support a bogus canal scheme in which she has heavily invested. Sir Robert, mostly reformed since his youth (and fortune), cannot accept such an exchange, but promises to do so in order to maintain his wife's faith in his moral inscrutability. Sir Robert appears willing to sacrifice anything to keep his wife's love, even a Cabinet seat. However, Lord Goring knows and Lady Chiltern has yet to learn that ambition, to Robert Chiltern, is as essential as air.

Lady Gertrude Chiltern: Although Lady Chiltern genuinely loves her husband, she is initially too obsessed with the idea of his perfection to realize that he may need her moral generosity more than her admiration. Lady Chiltern's idealization of duty and the expectations she holds for her husband are described as child-like, and even after her discovery and subsequent forgiveness of his past sins, she insists on his retirement from public service, believing that their love for each other will be enough to sustain them away from her husband's beloved London. Lady Chiltern's crucial moment of understanding occurs when Lord Goring quotes her the high price of a love that requires one to sacrifice too much.

Mrs. Cheveley: Mrs. Cheveley is the irredeemable villainess of the play. A life-long thief, she has appeared in London for the express purpose of blackmailing Robert Chiltern with his past. Spiteful and heartless to the last, Mrs. Cheveley first demands money from Sir Robert, then a marriage proposal from Lord Goring, whom she professes to love. At the refusal of both, she attempts to shatter Sir Robert's trust in his wife by misrepresenting a letter that Gertrude Chiltern wrote to Lord Goring, but due to a fortunate lack of thoroughness on her part, even this plan does not fulfill her malicious intentions.

Miss Mabel Chiltern: Sir Robert's sister. Miss Mabel takes the exercise of her wit quite seriously, using it to accommodate her intelligence to the frivolous Society in which she must thrive. Mabel is often quite outrageous, and approves of Lord Goring's dandyism just as vocally as his father disapproves of it. Her superficiality is her own high art, such that she effortlessly endears herself even to the usually disapproving Lord Caversham. Miss Mabel's most outrageous moment in the play occurs when Lord Goring professes his love for her and she promptly replies, "I know. And I think you might have mentioned it before. I am sure I have given you heaps of opportunities."

Lady Markby: A popular and matronly woman, she is the wife of a member of the House of Commons, who, in her opinion, is too devoted to his responsibilities. Lady Markby holds a great talent for including her husband in her complaints regarding the general state of the nation, and vice versa. She introduces Mrs. Cheveley into the Chilterns' party.

Vicomte de Nanjac: Attaché at French Embassy in London. He is an Anglophile of the highest order—and very little else.

Phipps: Lord Goring's servant, whose prompt "Yes, my lord"'s and deadpan pronouncements on Society make him an excellent member of Lord Goring's fashionable household. ❀

Critical Views on
An Ideal Husband

EPIFANIO SAN JUAN JR.: THE ACTION OF COMEDY

[Epifanio San Juan Jr. is professor and chair of the Department of Comparative American Cultures at Washington State University. He has also taught at the University of California, University of Connecticut, Brooklyn College of CUNY, and Tamkang University, Taiwan. His books include *The Art of Oscar Wilde, Beyond Postcolonial Theory, From Exile to Diaspora, After Postcolonialism,* and *The Racial Imaginary,* due out in 2001. This selection links Wilde's regard of fashion and politics as both disguises of reality.]

Dress or fashion furnishes an index to social attitudes and values. Lord Goring pronounces: "fashion is what one wears oneself. What is unfashionable is what other people wear." When he offers to give Mrs. Cheveley "some good advice," she replies: "Oh! Pray don't. One should never give a woman anything that she can't wear in the evening." The interest in appearance occupies the foreground in this exchange:

> MRS. CHEVELEY (*languidly*). I have never read a Blue Book. I prefer books . . . in yellow covers.
> LADY MARKBY (*genially unconscious*). Yellow is a gayer colour, is it not? I used to wear yellow a good deal in my early days, and would do so now if Sir John was not so painfully personal in his observations, and a man on the question of dress is always ridiculous, is he not?

Politics is a kind of "fashion," too, in its concern with public appearance. Lady Basildon claims to talk politics ceaselessly. Sir Robert Chiltern regards a political life as "a noble career," though our knowledge of his past belies his statement. But in the political or practical life, the criterion of success reduces moral standards to the basic level of pragmatic efficacy. As Lord Goring puts it, "in practical life there is something about success, actual success, that is a little unscrupulous, something about ambition that is unscrupulous always."

In Act IV, Lady Chiltern believes that Sir Robert's ambition has led him astray in his early days. She says that "power is nothing in itself. It is power to do good that is fine." Her husband admits to Lord Goring that he "bought success at a great price." And yet he is highly esteemed for being a respectable, selfless "public servant," a model of virtue, which is but a "front" or mask that he wears in conformity to social norms. After all, as Lord Goring remarks, almost all private fortune in society has come from dubious "speculation." On knowing her husband's guilt, Lady Chiltern hysterically complains not of his pretense but of his inability to "lie" to her for the sake of "virtues" he has been socially known for. Lady Chiltern cries out,

> Don't touch me. I feel as if you had soiled me forever. Oh! What a mask you have been wearing all these years! A horrible, painted mask! You sold yourself for money. Oh! A common thief were better. You put yourself up for sale to the highest bidder! You were bought in the market. You lied to the whole world. And yet you will not lie to me!

This exposure means a stripping of costume, an "undressing," to disclose the authentic self. One recalls Lady Markby's experience, which prefigures Sir Robert's plight, when she describes the result of immersion in the crowd:

> The fact is, we all scramble and jostle so much nowadays that I wonder we have anything at all left on us at the end of an evening. I know myself that, when I am coming back from the Drawing Room, I always feel as if I hadn't a shred on me, except a small shred of decent reputation just enough to prevent the lower classes making painful observations through the windows of the carriage. ⟨. . .⟩

The double aspects of life seem to be focused in Mrs. Cheveley's mysterious identity. Lord Goring describes her as "a genius in the daytime and a beauty at night." She plays with the attitudes of optimism and pessimism. What after all is the real self of a person? Lady Chiltern cannot believe her husband to be guilty of dreadful things which are "so unlike [his] real self." Her idealized image of him is that he has "brought into the political life of our time a nobler atmosphere, a finer attitude towards life, a freer air of purer aims and higher ideals." But reality is never as simple and pure as Lady Chiltern would like to imagine it. Society has become "dreadfully mixed" for Mrs. Cheveley; Lady Markby, likewise, observes that "families are so mixed nowadays. Indeed, as a rule, everybody turns out to be somebody else." Just as society is complex, so truth—as Sir Robert Chiltern believes—is a very complex thing. ⟨. . .⟩

Wilde describes the stage decoration in Act I: "Over the well of the staircase hangs a great chandelier with wax lights, which illumine a large eighteenth century French tapestry—representing the Triumph of Love, from a design by Boucher—that is stretched on the staircase wall." At the close of Act III, we see Mrs. Cheveley's face "illumined with evil triumph." What triumphs of course is the comic situation.

—Epifanio San Juan Jr., *The Art of Oscar Wilde* (Princeton, N.J.: Princeton University Press, 1967): pp. 167–177.

⁂

Alan Bird: Plot and Politics in *An Ideal Husband*

[Alan Bird is the author of *The Plays of Oscar Wilde* (1977). This selection questions apparent plot weaknesses in *An Ideal Husband* in favor for Wilde's social commentary regarding morality and corruption in modern politics.]

The plot of *An Ideal Husband* is not without its elements of improbability and, unlike *A Woman of No Importance,* is overloaded by an excessive number of reversals and twists. Sometimes the plot verges on the nonsensical. Why, for instance, should Mrs. Cheveley hand over to Lord Goring the compromising letter written by Sir Robert Chiltern because he would otherwise hand her over to the police as a thief and yet walk out of his house, undenounced, with the bracelet still clasped on her arm? Again, the credibility of Mrs. Cheveley's identity, like that of Mrs. Erlynne, is rather suspect; and it is difficult to believe that a woman who was at school with Lady Chiltern and engaged to be married to Lord Goring should not have been extremely well-known in the closely-knit fabric of London aristocratic society. There seems no need to have telegraphed Vienna for details of her later career since a woman who had been the mistress of an international financier, who had been immensely enriched after his death, who dabbled in international finance, and who still retained links with London society—with

Lady Markby at any rate—must have been recognized by many people. Unless Lord Goring is quite, quite old and, therefore, too old to become the husband of Mabel Chiltern, his engagement to Mrs. Cheveley must have been comparatively recent. And who was Mr. Cheveley—and how does he fit into the picture? The critic A. B. Walkley was quite right, when commenting on this play, to say that even Sardou had tired of kleptomania as a theatrical device; but it cannot be denied that Wilde uses the theft of the letter effectively. That there was a similarity between Sardou's *Dora* and *An Ideal Husband* is undeniable, but a play can be interesting to the ordinary playgoer even if the plot is not particularly original: as with Shakespeare, originality of plot, similarity of structure, and the use of dramatic devices of a conventional nature are matters which concern professional critics and scholars rather than the public which, by and large, wishes to be interested and entertained.

Not unexpectedly, despite the fact that the critics charged him with having stolen his adventures from Augier and his tirades from Dumas *fils*, they did not comment on those elements of the play which were individual to Wilde, notably the political background which he treated in an ironical, cynical way which was quite unique for the period. It is arguably the most serious of Wilde's social comedies, not because of its exploitation of the woman with a 'past', but because of its political overtones. In his criticism of the play A. B. Walkley stated that its plot was incredible because it was most improbable that any of the politicians of the day would behave in such a way: 'When Bulwer Lytton and Disraeli wrote novels picturing politics as a drawing-room game of this kind, they only distorted, not actually falsified, the facts,' he stated, and added, 'But nowadays, of course, such a picture is stark, staring nonsense' (Review signed A. B. W. in *Speaker,* 12 January 1895). The plain fact of the matter is that Wilde was guilty of hardly any exaggeration, as political historians would and should be the first to admit.

In the play Mrs. Cheveley tries to force Sir Robert Chiltern's hand by threatening to reveal that he divulged the secret that the British Government, of which he was a junior member, intended to purchase Suez Canal shares, mercenary conduct on the part of a civil servant which must have seemed impossible to innocent dramatic and literary journalists. Historians, however, have always known that the sources of all great wealth are vicious, tainted and corrupt. What the public of

Wilde's day did not know was that Disraeli had been forced to borrow money from the Rothschilds in order to finance the government's purchase of Suez Canal shares and that this deal must certainly have strengthened the hands (and enlarged the funds) of the dealers in these and related shares. And this furtive financial intrigue had taken place only twenty years or so before *An Ideal Husband* had been written. The Prince of Wales himself relied heavily for his financial support on such men as the (imaginary) Baron Arnheim; his own chief supporters from whom he borrowed heavily were the financiers Baron Hirsch and Sir Ernest Cassell. It is said that at a ball the Prince of Wales playfully asked the lady with whom he was dancing, 'And now, what does Lady Salome want?' To which she replied, 'The head of Sir Ernest, sire.' At which the Prince stalked away in indignation. The financial adventures of Rhodes and other international crooks in Southern Africa was as skilfully veiled behind a patriotic flag in Wilde's day as it is in ours. In the second half of the nineteenth century the world of European finance, whether of notorious barons in Vienna or anonymous gnomes in Zurich, had begun to intrude more and more upon domestic politics. ⟨. . .⟩

What Wilde demonstrates in this play is that the great secret of public success is simply never to be found out. *An Ideal Husband* does, in fact, enable us to rejoice over the escape of a sinner from the penalty of his sin through the trick of his friend with the diamond brooch-bracelet. This is not a convincing trick; and, perhaps, Wilde did not seriously intend it to be so. The action demonstrates the basic hypocrisy of English life. Mrs. Cheveley may seem to represent international and amoral finance forcing its way into English society and public life; but there can be no doubt that the ground had been well tilled and was ready for her activities. A further twist is given by the fact that Mrs. Cheveley is not actually an intruder—by birth and upbringing she is a member of English society and is, as the reply to Sir Robert's telegram to the Embassy at Vienna demonstrates, a leading and perfectly respectable member of society there, too. And Vienna under the Emperor Franz Joseph was, if anything, infinitely more rigid and righteous in its morality than was London. Mrs. Cheveley moves gracefully in both societies, in both capitals. Wilde could take dramatic cynicism no further.

—Alan Bird, *The Plays of Oscar Wilde* (London, England: Vision Press Limited, 1977): pp. 143–145, 149.

IAN SMALL: SEMIOTICS AND OSCAR'S WILDE'S ACCOUNTS OF ART

[Ian Small has written *Conditions for Criticism, Politics & Value in English Studies,* and *Oscar Wilde's Profession.* He has also edited and authored introductions for numerous volumes of works by Wilde, Yeats, R. K. Thornton, Johnson, and others. In this essay, Small emphasizes the significance of objects on the Wildean stage.]

⟨. . .⟩ Wilde more than any figure in the last decades of the nineteenth century knew of the way a man's possessions spoke for him. The Louis Seize cane or furniture, the gold-tipped cigarettes, the carefully selected button-hole were possessions that spoke for Wilde and for the central characters in his social dramas. But what best announces to the world the tastes and values of the clever man are the art objects he selects: they locate him in political and social spheres. In *The Picture of Dorian Gray* Dorian's and Lord Henry's connoisseurship defines how they are placed in the power structures of nineteenth-century society generally. In this respect Wilde's most interesting work is *An Ideal Husband.* In the first act Wilde introduces his characters by describing them, in the stage directions of the first printed edition of the play, in terms of their most appropriate portraitists. The artists mentioned are Boucher, Watteau, Lawrence and Van Dyck. Wilde is designating aspects of character by reference to the cultural significance that attaches to the work of specific painters and by extension locating those characters on a social and political (as well as a dramatic) spectrum of values. The pictures are not operating as graphic or iconic signs within an aesthetic code but within other social codes. The central contrast is a political one and is between Van Dyck, the putative portraitist of Sir Robert Chiltern, the play's main character, and Watteau, used to depict two minor female characters of great prettiness and "exquisite fragility." Some of the relevant passages from the stage-directions are these: "*Sir Robert Chiltern . . . A personality of mark. Not popular— few personalities are. But intensely admired by the few, and deeply respected by the many . . . It would be inaccurate to call him picturesque. Picturesqueness cannot survive the House of Commons. But Van Dyck would have loved to paint his head.*" Earlier Mabel Chiltern's modernity is characterized by her being compared to a (recently discovered) Tanagra statuette and Mrs. Cheveley, clearly marked out as a "fast" and thus socially dangerous woman, is "a work of art, on the whole, but showing the influence of too many schools." A nineteenth-century reading public would quite clearly grasp the distinction between the established portraitist, connoting order, tradition and authority, the gentle pastoralism of Watteau, suggestive, to the Decadent sensibility, of a delicate eroticism, the modernity of a Tanagra statuette and a style-less eclecticism. The art objects that Wilde selects, that is, themselves implicate the political values that are central to the play's development.

If such an account of Wilde has any merit it is to suggest that the taxonomy of modes of writing and pictorial representation that sets the "modernist" against the "Victorian" *solely* in terms of a critique of the concept of representation is misplaced. Such a view is true, but only partly so. Wilde's *oeuvre* suggests that early modernists well knew that pictorial or literary art could embody interpretative "openness" and thus invite questions about their functions as representation; but that they also knew that these features in themselves did not prevent art objects from being assigned specific social value or being used with a specific social function.

—Ian Small, "Semiotics and Oscar Wilde's Accounts of Art," *British Journal of Aesthetics* 25, no. 1 (Winter 1985): pp. 50–56.

PETER RABY: ACHIEVING PLAY

[Peter Raby is the editor of several volumes of Oscar Wilde. He has also written *Alfred Russel Wallace: A Life, Bright Paradise, The Way of All Flesh, Aubrey Beardsley and the Nineties, Samuel Butler: A Biography,* and The Importance of Being Earnest: *A Reader's Companion.* In this selection, Raby admires Wilde's characterization of Lord Goring, who is both a perfect dandy and serious wit.]

The playfulness which surrounds Lord Goring is one of Wilde's most assured achievements. In *Lady Windermere's Fan* he had difficulty in reconciling the witty Lord Darlington with the serious lover; in *A Woman of No Importance* he struggled with the problem of the callous dandy; here he contrives to distance Lord Goring by matching him with an apparently frivolous, witty and unsentimental heroine. From time to time, indeed, the play comes to a virtual standstill while usually Lord Goring, less often some other of the 'trivial' characters, are allowed to play purely with words. Mrs Marchmont and Lady Basildon, Mabel Chiltern and Lord Caversham, provide a vein of light wit which encapsulates the unserious love-match, the counterpoint to the Chiltern's earnest marriage:

> MABEL CHILTERN: You are always telling me your bad qualities, Lord Goring.
> LORD GORING: I have only told you half of them as yet, Miss Mabel!
> MABEL CHILTERN: Are the others very bad?
> LORD GORING: Quite dreadful! When I think of them at night I go to sleep at once.
> MABEL CHILTERN: Well, I delight in your bad qualities. I wouldn't have you part with one of them.

This shared mask of frivolity, a preliminary sketch for Cecily and Algernon, serves as a refreshing contrast to the solemnity of Lady Chiltern's attitude to life. It recurs later in the same act when Lord Goring takes charge of the diamond brooch:

> LORD GORING: I am going to make a rather strange request of you, Miss Mabel.
> MABEL CHILTERN [*eagerly*]: Oh, pray do! I have been waiting for it all the evening.

This is Wilde inclining towards a new kind of comedy in his knowing manipulation of dramatic convention. Another passage where Wilde seems on the point of modulating into a different genre is at the opening of Act Four:

> LORD GORING [*pulls out his watch, inspects it, and rings the bell*]: It is a great nuisance. I can't find anyone in this house to talk to. And I am full of interesting information. I feel like the latest edition of something or other.

Lord Goring, one feels, needs to be in another play to find someone suitable to talk to (apart from himself, or his author, to whom he bears a striking resemblance). But the classic location is the opening exchange between him and the Ideal Butler, Phipps, who 'represents the dominance of form':

LORD GORING: For the future a more trivial buttonhole, Phipps, on Thursday evenings.

PHIPPS: I will speak to the florist, my lord. She has had a loss in her family lately, which perhaps accounts for the lack of triviality your lordship complains of in the buttonhole.

LORD GORING: Extraordinary thing about the lower classes in England—they are always losing their relations.

PHIPPS: Yes, my lord. They are extremely fortunate in that respect.

This conversation begins to establish a comic style and ambiance which Wilde eventually contrives to subordinate to the world of international finance and the Foreign Office, but only with a sense of loss. The play, as a well-constructed vehicle, functions adequately. The mechanical elements, the pair of letters, even the diamond brooch which Lord Goring transforms into a manacling bracelet, need not obtrude unduly, especially if they are handled as delicately as Wilde doubtless intended. Only the too-convenient falling of the chair in Act Three, as Shaw noted, betrays Wilde in an uncharacteristic carelessness. Yet it is the sub-plot, and the sub-text, with its increasingly insistent emphasis on form and style, which give the play its chief distinction and delight.

The contemporary, political glances are not nearly so far-fetched as some reviewers suggested, especially if they are approached as representative, even metaphoric, rather than as narrowly realistic. The use which David Hare and Howard Brenton make of political structures and events in *Pravda* is not dissimilar; and once again, the plays of Ibsen come to mind, for example *The Pillars of Society*. There is a greater assurance and sharpness in *An Ideal Husband*, generated in part no doubt by Wilde's growing confidence, in part by a sense of new developments in English contemporary drama. Pinero's *The Second Mrs Tanqueray* had appeared in June 1893, while Wilde had admired Shaw's *Widower's Houses* and his 'superb confidence in the dramatic value of the mere facts of life'. It may have been partly a self-protective gesture which led Shaw to emphasise the 'subtle and pervading levity' of *An Ideal Husband*, and to protest that it was 'useless to describe a play which has no thesis: which is, in the purest integrity, a play and nothing less'. When Wilde proceeded to create a 'pure' play, with *The Importance of Being Earnest*, Shaw complained that it had no heart. *An Ideal Husband* contrives to remain, like its ending, lightly equivocal, suggesting a thesis but refusing to state it.

—Peter Raby, *Oscar Wilde* (Cambridge, England: Cambridge University Press, 1988): pp. 98–100.

☙

Patricia Flanagan Behrendt: The Dandy Coup de Théâtre

[Patricia Flanagan Behrendt, assistant professor of theatre arts and dance at the University of Nebraska-Lincoln, is the author of *Oscar Wilde: Eros and Aesthetics* (1991). In this excerpt, Behrendt discusses Wilde's literary ambition for his dandy characters beyond mere fashionable aesthetic.]

In 1966, Ian Gregor, who has recognized many of the darker themes in Wilde's plays, suggested that the faults in the plays derive from Wilde's preoccupation with creating a satisfactory realization of the dandy character. Gregor concludes that

> The involvement [of the dandy] of one kind or another was the root defect of these plays, and in writing his third play, *An Ideal Husband,* Wilde seemed to have taken special care to keep his dandy free from commitment. If Lord Goring is to be in love it will be with a minor figure of the play, and his 'love' will simply be there to testify to his status as hero. His connection with the central figure of the play [Lord Chiltern] will not be a profoundly emotional one, and will not involve him with a woman, faithfully or otherwise. And so we find Wilde giving Goring a friendship with Sir Robert Chiltern and hoping that the dandy, limited to the more fitting role of guide and philosopher, will at last find insurance against loss of wit.

Gregor's observations about the development of Wilde's dandy character, however, overlook the fact that Wilde's pursuit of a "clearer insight into the dramatic requirements of the dandy" was a far cry from the average task of the playwright confronting a problem in the craft. Wilde's task as playwright was to conceal as much as—if not more than—he reveals. After all, his treatment of homosexual Eros, which I have shown to be a significant component of the dandy role, could never aspire to the Victorian stage undisguised.

Gregor's criticism of Wilde's plays concludes that their defects arise from Wilde's attempts to "realize the significance of the dandy in appropriate action. In *Lady Windermere's Fan* he had become a sympathetic lover and had been rendered null; in *A Woman of No Importance* he has been a faithless lover and is degraded into a melodramatic villain." However, as I have demonstrated, the role of the dandy in these earlier plays is neither that of the "sympathetic lover . . . rendered null" nor that of a character reduced to the role of "melodramatic villain." In assuming that Wilde was struggling to realize the dandy "in an appropriate action," Gregor fails to consider that Wilde purposefully placed the dandy in specific situations designed to reveal the impossibility of certain actions or relationships on the part of the dandy for reasons clearly understood by the homosexual subculture in Wilde's audience.

The dandy embodies Wilde's vision of the homosexual intellectual who demonstrates his superiority in his ability to manipulate and to predict the actions of others and in his ability to seek experience for the sake of experience, while avoiding entrapment by the conventions of a society whose values he repudiates. Lord Darlington enjoyed his pursuit of Lady Windermere as an intellectual exercise. Through Darlington's machinations, Wilde reveals the hypocrisy of marriages based upon the need for deception and lies. Lord Illingworth intrudes into the relationship between mother and son. While he departs seemingly with nothing for his labors, Wilde has used him to reveal the cloying nature of the repressive relationship between mother and son which one cannot help but feel that Illingworth is "well out of."

In *An Ideal Husband*, Wilde presents a dandy, Lord Goring, whose interference in the affairs of another man creates a bond between them. Unlike Wilde's earlier plays, in which the dandy's involvement was primarily with a younger disciple whom he would remold in his own image, *An Ideal Husband* presents a more mature relationship between two men who are closer in age. In an effort to protect the career interests of Goring's friend, Sir Robert Chiltern, Wilde finally allows his dandy—as we will see—fully to articulate his actual contempt for women.

—Patricia Flanagan Behrendt, *Oscar Wilde: Eros and Aesthetics*
(London, England: Macmillan Academic and Professional Ltd, 1991):
pp. 159–161.

SOS ELTIS: WILDE'S IDEAL SINNER

[Sos Eltis has taught at St. John's College, Oxford, and Boston
University. He is currently a Fellow in English at Brasenose
College, Oxford. This essay focuses on Wilde's implicit criti-
cism of nineteenth-century politics in *An Ideal Husband*.]

In the final published version of *An Ideal Husband*, Sir Robert
Chiltern is the vehicle for Wilde's implicit criticism of nineteenth-
century politics. This ambitious and unscrupulous politician, whose
entire career is based upon his reputation for upright character and
unshakeable honesty, is not only rewarded with a seat in the Cabinet,
but backed as a possible future leader for the country. Lord Caversham declares that "If the country doesn't go to the dogs or the Rad-
icals, we shall have you Prime Minister, some day.' The play's happy
ending consists of the entry into the inner sanctum of the British
government of a man who, without regrets, sold his political
integrity for personal gain. No contemporary reviewer expressed
outrage or disbelief at such a conclusion, though some of them
observed mildly that Wilde's statesman seemed well rewarded for his
lack of principle. The very fact that the audience accepted the play's
ending so easily demonstrates Wilde's success in portraying British
politics as a scene of compromise and hypocrisy, where Sir Robert
will be perfectly at home.

The ironic view of contemporary politics implicit in this ending
was more directly expressed in earlier drafts of the play. In the final
version Mrs Cheveley undercuts Sir Robert's exclamation that, 'A
political life is a noble career!', by replying 'Sometimes. And sometimes it is a clever game, Sir Robert.' In the first manuscript draft of
the play she further degrades the statesman's standing:

MRS CHEVELEY: But one must amuse oneself somehow. And I like
the gambling element in politics.
SIR ROBERT: You would sooner play with people than with cards.

Sir Robert accepts instantly Mrs Cheveley's cynical description of the political game.

Sir Robert Chiltern's guilty secret implicates the rest of society. He cannot feel remorse, for he knows his crime is sanctioned by common usage. As he explains to Goring: 'I felt that I had fought the century with its own weapons and won.' In the first manuscript draft, Sir Robert's sin is symptomatic of his society. Mrs Cheveley relates how she discovered a veritable treasure-trove of corruption in the dead Baron's escritoire:

> The secret history of the nineteenth century was in it. Letters from great ladies offering their favours for money. Letters from great men offering their support for money. Letters from kings who had lost their thrones. Letters from demagogues who wanted to be kings. And a letter from you on the top of which, in that small delicate hand of his that you must remember, the Baron had written 'the origin of Sir Robert Chiltern'—and on the back of it the sum £50,000. ⟨. . .⟩

This subtle process of introducing satire through character rather than through more overt statements is also seen at work in Sir Robert Chiltern. Through successive drafts, Wilde camouflaged his social criticisms, while simultaneously widening and strengthening their implications. In the earlier drafts the play Sir Robert is a considerably more unscrupulous and self-interested character. It was Lord Caversham, and not the unseen Lord Radley, who employed him and whose confidence he betrayed, a fact which makes his treachery seem deeper and more personal. He agrees to Mrs Cheveley's demands with undignified rapidity. The details of his impoverished and undignified past elicit the audience's sympathy, but they also present Sir Robert as himself a proponent of nineteenth-century materialism and snobbery. Everybody has their price, Mrs Cheveley declares: 'The drawback is that most people are so dreadfully expensive.' Sir Robert's price is raised from £50,000 in the first draft, to £85,000, and finally £110,000.

It is not just that a higher value is placed on his integrity, however, for by the final version Sir Robert has been transformed from a product of the nineteenth century into a critic of it. Not only does he use the century's own weapons against itself, he challenges its entire moral ethos:

> Weak? Oh, I am sick of hearing that phrase. Sick of using it
> of others. Weak! Do you really think, Arthur, that it is
> weakness that yields to temptation? I tell you that there are
> terrible temptations that it requires strength, strength and
> courage to yield to. To stake all one's life on a single
> moment, to risk everything on one throw, whether the
> stake be power or pleasure, I care not—there is no weak-
> ness in that. There is a horrible, a terrible courage. I had
> that courage.

Shaw, in his review, picked out this speech for praise as striking 'the modern note'. In the final version Sir Robert develops from a man who is simply concerned with gaining the place in society to which his birth entitles him into a man who is driven by a personal creed of self-realization and success. So Baron Arnheim's philosophy is expanded and explained by Sir Robert: '[P]ower, power over other men, power over the world, was the one thing worth having, the one supreme pleasure worth knowing, the one joy one never tired of, and that in our century only the rich possessed it.' The effect of these revisions is to make Sir Robert a rebel. His crime still implicates society in the combination of materialism and snobbery that drove him to the deed. Yet, by separating Sir Robert from the ethics of his century, Wilde makes his statesman not inferior to the system he betrays but superior to it. Sir Robert is no longer a product of his century; he is a critic of it, a critic who exploits its faults and uses them against it. Sir Robert follows the strictures of 'The Soul of Man', in which Wilde proclaimed:

> Disobedience, in the eyes of anyone who has read history,
> is man's original virtue. It is through disobedience that
> progress has been made, through disobedience and
> through rebellion . . . No: a poor man who is ungrateful,
> unthrifty, discontented and rebellious, is probably a real
> personality, and has much in him. He is at any rate a
> healthy protest.

Sir Robert may not be poor by socialist standards, but by his own assessment he is, and his reaction is to rebel against the system which made him so. Sir Robert is transformed from an uninteresting modern criminal who simply steals for money into a true individualist, who sins in remaining true to his own ethos. This is a completely different matter, for, as Wilde writes of the true personality,

'He may commit a sin against society, and yet realize through that sin his true perfection.'

—Sos Eltis, *Revising Wilde: Society and Subversion in the Plays of Oscar Wilde* (Oxford, England: Clarendon Press, 1996): pp. 135–139.

Plot Summary of
Lady Windermere's Fan

When Margaret Windermere rebukes Lord Darlington for paying her too many compliments, there is nothing coquettish in her protests at all. She is in earnest, as she is in identifying herself as a sort of Puritan. For this young wife who has just only come of age, the divide between good and bad seems as clear as the line marking the horizon of a clear day, and she becomes only more irritated at the well-meaning Darlington on his apparent moral flippancy when he proclaims: "Oh, now-a-days so many conceited people go about society pretending to be good, that I think it shows rather a sweet and modest disposition to pretend to be bad." Here is the heart of the play and playwright alike: that social definitions are only as 'good' as the people that make them in the first place, and that these definitions are quite as arbitrary, or even blatantly counterintuitive, as Society's sense of fashion. Certainly, Wilde and any of his wickedly intelligent dandies knew the game of Fashion and played it impeccably, and it is to his (and their credit) that they try to lend the sharpness of their vision to others who stubbornly insist on blindness.

Lord Darlington is the first to warn Lady Windermere of her husband's indiscretion regarding his interactions with Mrs. Erlynne, who, as far as Society is concerned, appears to be his mistress. The naïve wife, very much in love and loved by her husband, refuses to even consider Lord Darlington's intimation as what it is, and continues tending to her parlor flowers. The Duchess of Berwick is quite less subtle. Insisting that "the whole of London knows it," the Duchess blithely advises the younger woman to take her husband away from the city for a vacation so as to discretely remove him from the offending woman. The Duchess' utter void of sensibility of her hostess' distress and some sense of reality in general—made plain by her constant reference to the "clever talk" of her daughter, Agatha, who speaks only the two words, "Yes, Mamma," throughout the play—seems to validate Lord Darlington's earlier statement that life should not be talked "seriously" about, for it is far too important. The Duchess believes that she is speaking seriously to her regrettably innocent friend; in such a case, Lord Darlington is right that Society should not attempt such things.

In the close of the **first act**, we, together with Lady Windermere, can only feel outrage at the response of Lord Windermere to his wife's demand for an explanation. He offers no explanation except denial, and adds insult to injury by insisting that Margaret invite Mrs. Erlynne to her birthday party later that evening. At her refusal, he does the unthinkable and extends the invitation herself, directly in the face of her threats against him if he would not respect her wishes. At the ball, even the men, Lord Windermere's closest friends, express uneasiness regarding his relations with the mysterious new-comer. Lord Augustus appears particularly anxious, for he, hope-lessly infatuated with her already, is personally invested in Mrs. Erlynne's social acceptability: "Hem! Well, look here, dear old fellow. Do you think she will ever get into this demmed thing called Society? Would you introduce her to your wife? No use beating about the confounded bush. Would you do that?" Wilde subtitled his masterpiece *The Importance of Being Earnest,* "A Trivial Comedy for Serious People," and his plays are richly supplied with such person-ages—serious people who use comedy to avert Society's gaze from their brilliance. Not unfortunately, either for him or for us as readers, Lord Augustus is decisively not of that cast. His comedy, as his person in full, is strictly trivial; his recognition of Society as "this demmed thing" is the result of an exasperated intelligence in the most literal sense—for his flashes of insight occur purely inci-dentally, as if his inner sensibility were sorely exasperated at its mental housing in the endearingly coarse and gullible "Tuppy." But Mrs. Erlynne is determined to infiltrate "this demmed thing," and the amiable—and perhaps more importantly, wealthy—Lord Augustus provides the perfect match.

Mrs. Erlynne, the type of woman that "forms the basis of other people's marriages" by properly distracting the men from being unfashionably faithful to their wives, charms men and women alike at the Windermere party, and Lady Windermere, painfully naïve and revealing a latent inclination for melodrama, cannot completely dis-count Lord Darlington's proposition that she run away with him that night. Leaving her husband a letter indicating her departure on the table, she gathers her cloak in a not-quite becoming flurry of theatricality for her nighttime visit to Lord Darlington.

It is at the moment of Margaret's greatest physical and moral vul-nerability that she is saved by the person she considers her greatest enemy. Mrs. Erlynne discovers the letter before it is read by Windermere, reveals to the audience her true identity as Margaret Windermere's mother, and passionately vows that she will save her daughter from repeating the mistake that caused the ruin of her own life some twenty years before. The scorned woman turned mother is a crucial twist in the dramatic action of the play, which, in order to fulfill the order implied by Lord Darlington in its beginning lines, requires a higher emotion than Lady Windermere's misplaced hysteria. This hysteria, merely a manifestation of Margaret's earlier Puritanical notions of purity and moral perfection, only confirms her mental limitations, whereas the possibility of transformation—that of perspective—throws light upon the ambiguity of goodness introduced to her by Lord Darlington. Lord Darlington declines rapidly in dramatic usefulness after the second act. His famous "I can resist everything except temptation" uttered in the first act serves as the eventual death sentence of his character, which having recklessly offered himself to temptation, cannot be sustained, for Lady Windermere can very well resist temptation, including the temptation of temptation, temptation's highest form.

The significance of the title fan shifts with its every appearance in the play. Its first occurrence in the receiving room of the Windermeres, the personalized fan, the birthday present of Arthur to Margaret Windermere, lies on a table, possibly next to a vase of roses that its owner is arranging, and provides the perfect accessory to the perfect scene of the perfect wife in the perfect home. Next, the fan is Lady Windermere's failed weapon of apparently failed domesticity. Margaret had resolved that she would strike the sinning woman with the fan if she dared to enter the house, but finds that she cannot; the fan literally and figuratively drops, harmless, to the floor. In **Act III**, the fan becomes the crucial prop to the advancement of the plot. The two women, cornered at Lord Darlington's house, cannot afford to be seen at such an hour in this famous bachelor's chambers. Yet both women may have safely avoided detection, if Lady Windermere had not left behind her fan, which alerts the other men to sportingly confront Darlington on who he has been entertaining in his room. When Arthur Windermere recognizes the fan as his wife's and angrily demands an explanation from Darlington, Mrs. Erlynne steps out from her hiding place and claims the fan as her mistake in having taken the thing as her own when leaving the Windermere's party. The maternal instinct that has led her to her daughter's side in the first place makes yet another leap on Margaret's behalf.

Still, as both Arthur Windermere and his newly-discovered mother-in-law instinctively understand, Margaret Windermere does better to continue to kneel at the shrine of her 'dead' mother than to know the real flesh-and-blood woman who gave birth to her and subsequently abandoned both daughter and social propriety in her own selfishness. The only connection, save one, that may be allowed to exist between mother and daughter, then, is the fan, inscribed with their common name, Margaret. The other is their common secret of Lord Darlington's almost-successful proposition. That also, like the fan, passes from the younger to older Margaret, never to be seen or spoken of again. ❀

List of Characters in
Lady Windermere's Fan

Lord (Arthur) Windermere: Lord Windermere is highly esteemed by all who know him, yet he seems recently to have embroiled himself in a compromising situation with a disreputable woman, Mrs. Erlynne. Arthur genuinely loves his wife, and the nature of his involvement with Mrs. Erlynne is not as it may appear, for the true identity of this woman threatens Lady Windermere's understanding of her past, and Arthur believes that he must do everything in his power to protect his wife from discovering the truth about Mrs. Erlynne. Still, Arthur's devotion to his wife depends on the strength of her moral purity, and he remains largely unknowing of his wife's critical development by the end of the play.

Lady (Margaret) Windermere: Arthur Windermere's young wife, who is much loved and respected by Society. She describes herself as somewhat Puritanical, as she was raised by a stern aunt in the early absence of her mother. At the play's opening, Lady Windermere's adherence to a rigid and unforgiving system of morality is emphasized, especially as she subsequently begins to suspect her husband of an illicit affair. Feeling herself terribly betrayed, the naïve Margaret turns to Lord Darlington with an intention for retribution. She does not ultimately act upon her impulse, but the experience teaches Margaret that morality, like people, cannot be set in black and white, good or evil.

Lord Darlington: A close friend of Lord Windermere, Lord Darlington is a devoted dandy. Still, true to the Wildean form, Darlington is by no means unintelligent, and he is the first to try to warn Lady Windermere of the rumors surrounding her husband's relations with Mrs. Erlynne. Darlington's critical downfall occurs when his devotion to his friend and dandyism becomes eclipsed by an emerging devotion for the newly distressed Margaret, whom he passionately—and almost successfully—propositions. However, when his hopes for romance ultimately fail, Lord Darlington becomes a deflated and dramatically useless character, and leaves London.

Mrs. Erlynne: A mysterious new addition to London Society, Mrs. Erlynne is a skillful social climber, who has manipulated both Lord

Windermere and Lord Augustus to serve her purposes. Yet despite all appearances, Mrs. Erlynne is merely pragmatic, and does not intend any real harm. Only Lord Windermere knows her true identity—she is Margaret's birth mother, whom she believes has been dead for close to two decades, but who actually abandoned her infant daughter with her lover. Knowing well the moral temperament of the Winderemeres, Mrs. Erlynne blackmails Arthur to provide for her social aspiration, in return for her keeping her shameful identity undisclosed to her naïve daughter. Mrs. Erlynne has hardly reformed, but she does experience one moment of maternal sacrifice, when she intercepts Lady Windermere from compromising herself with Lord Darlington.

Lord Augustus Lorton: Self-proclaimed the "most good-natured man in London," Lord Augustus is an endearingly bumbling, and often bewildered, gentleman, who is much infatuated with Mrs. Erlynne. He is easily swayed by her quick explanations, and will be her future husband.

The Duchess of Berwick: Duchess Berwick is the epitome of the over-civilized Society lady. With her highly marriageable daughter, Agatha, in tow, the Duchess calls from well-heeled house to house to chatter in the high irrelevance and irreverence of the time. The Duchess of Berwick is Lord Augustus' sister.

Lady Agatha Carlisle: The Duchess's daughter, Agatha is an almost painfully comic character, whose only utterance through the play is the ubiquitous "Yes, mamma." To the delight of the Duchess, she becomes betrothed to the Australian gentleman, Mr. Hopper. ❀

Critical Views on
Lady Windermere's Fan

PHILIP K. COHEN: THE MORAL VISION OF
OSCAR WILDE

[Philip K. Cohen is the author of *The Moral Vision of Oscar Wilde* (1978). He is a member of the Maryland State Department of Education. In this selection, Cohen discusses the moral and literary reversals in both the characters and the readers of the play.]

Wilde structures *Lady Windermere's Fan* upon the principle of reversal. During the course of the play, he reverses the reader's attitude toward Mrs. Erlynne, initially the subject of intense dislike. And Lady Windermere, who at first seems an idealized portrait of virtue, diminishes in esteem as the play progresses. Mrs. Erlynne enters as the potential destroyer of a marriage and exists as the party solely responsible for its preservation. At the outset, she wants Lady Windermere to help her "get back." But at the climax of the play, she helps her daughter to stay in society. She accepts public disgrace in Darlington's rooms in order to save Margaret, who planned to shame her at the birthday celebration. The adventuress who blackmails Windermere with the threat of revealing a secret exerts her power over him and his wife in the end to assure that two secrets will be kept. Wilde enforces these reversals with still further turnabouts. Margaret, who despises Mrs. Erlynne at the outset, admires her in the end. Windermere, who at first thought her a woman more sinned against than sinning, comes to consider her absolutely evil and retains this opinion until the last seconds of act 4. In act 1 he ignored his wife's prohibition by inviting Mrs. Erlynne to their home. In the last act, Lady Windermere overrides her husband's prohibition by inviting the same woman to enter their residence.

The play's reversals accord thoroughly with Wilde's rigorous moral argument. It has been asserted that he seeks to expose the inadequacy of moral absolutes. But, as has been shown in the treatment of *Salomé,* he clung tenaciously to them even when the necessary order they supplied brought with it intolerable guilt and anxiety. In the first act, Lady Windermere champions "what the world is forgetting, the difference that there is between what is right and what is wrong. *She* [i.e., her aunt] allowed of no compromise. *I* allow of none." Nor does Wilde. She enunciates the values against which all the characters, herself included, are to be judged:

> Nowadays people seem to look on life as a speculation. It is not a speculation. It is a sacrament. Its ideal is Love. Its purification is sacrifice. ⟨. . .⟩

But, if only for a few hours, Lady Windermere does reject her maternal obligations. She, who has espoused "the ideal of love," goes to a man she does not love. This act demonstrates her incapacity for sacrifice, which she has identified as the "purification" of the "sacrament" of life. She fails equally to attain Darlington's opposing—and lesser—ideal of absolute individualism. Rather than gaining complete control over her destiny and seeking untrammeled self-realization, she forsakes a seemingly ignoble surrender of selfhood for one that is genuinely so:

> Which is the worst, I wonder, to be at the mercy of a man who loves one, or the wife of a man who in one's own house dishonours one? . . . But will he love me always, this man to whom I am giving my life?

But Mrs. Erlynne, who opposes Darlington in the moral debate, saves her pathetic daughter from having to answer such questions. ⟨. . .⟩

But Mrs. Erlynne and the audience have achieved an awareness beside which Margaret Windermere's seems only a small first step. She will never learn Mrs. Erlynne's true identity. Nor will her husband even discover her temporary desertion. And Darlington, who canonizes Margaret for rejecting him, has erected a false ideal of his own. He, who began as an opportunist, ends as a sentimental idealist. He, who told Margaret that people are either charming or not and rejected moral criteria, now sees her as an absolutely pure and good woman. She knows that she is not, but neither he nor her husband will share this knowledge. The force of illusion, which Wilde links to conventional idealism, is summed up in Margaret's feelings toward her supposedly dead mother. She refuses to adapt these feelings to her newly acquired insight into human nature. Although she can now forgive, she insists on believing in one person who is perfect and therefore beyond the need for mercy:

LADY WINDERMERE. We all have ideals in life. At least we all should
    have. Mine is my mother.
MRS. ERLYNNE. Ideals are dangerous things. Realities are better.
    They wound, but they're better.
LADY WINDERMERE. If I lost my ideals, I should lose everything.

The audience and Mrs. Erlynne recognize the sad truth in what she
says.

—Philip K. Cohen, *The Moral Vision of Oscar Wilde* (Madison, N.J.:
Fairleigh Dickinson University Press, 1978): pp. 184–185, 187–190.

⊗

PETER RABY: SOCIETY AND THE SEXUAL MARKETPLACE IN WILDE'S LONDON

[Peter Raby is the editor of several volumes of Oscar Wilde.
He has also written *Alfred Russel Wallace: A Life, Bright Paradise, The Way of All Flesh, Aubrey Beardsley and the
Nineties, Samuel Butler: A Biography,* and The Importance
of Being Earnest: *A Reader's Companion.* This excerpt discusses the trades of marriage, sexuality and fashion in
Wilde's social comedies.]

Society, and its London centerpiece the season, is depicted as a
sexual market-place. There are three major sexual encounters surrounding the Windermeres' marriage: Lord Darlington's pursuit of
Lady Windermere (justified on the grounds that Windermere has
broken the bonds of marriage and so set her free, thought Windermere's interest in Mrs Erlynne is not, of course, what it seems); Mrs
Erlynne's pursuit of Lord Augustus; and Lady Agatha's mother-directed quest for Mr Hopper. These three encounters are placed in
the glittering context of the Windermeres' 'small and early' dance,
and the superficiality of the values which inform such functions is
both implicitly and explicitly exposed. There are light economic
vignettes; such as the ingratiating Dumby, whose prototype was presumably applauding from the stalls:

DUMBY: Good evening, Lady Stutfield. I suppose this will be the
    last ball of the season?

LADY STUTFIELD: I suppose so, Mr Dumby. It's been a delightful
    season, hasn't it?
DUMBY: Quite delightful! Good evening, Duchess. I suppose this
    will be the last ball of the season?
DUCHESS OF BERWICK: I suppose so, Mr Dumby. It has been a very
    dull season, hasn't it?
DUMBY: Dreadfully dull! Dreadfully dull!
MRS COWPER-COWPER: Good evening, Mr Dumby. I suppose this
    will be the last ball of the season?
DUMBY: Oh I think not. There'll probably be two more.

More pointedly, there is the Duchess of Berwick's campaign to marry her complaisant daughter Lady Agatha to the wealthy Australian—'Ah, we know your value, Mr Hopper. We wish there were more like you'—which is satisfactorily accomplished by the end of the ball, and which serves as an echo of the maturer hunting of Lord Augustus by Mrs Erlynne and also, perhaps, of the earlier match between the Windermeres. The most telling critiques are those which are only implied: for instance, Mrs Erlynne's ability to blackmail Lord Windermere because of the shock which the truth might give to her daughter. Reminiscent in places of the fairy-stories, the comedies develop their own kind of oblique moral commentary. A world which must have seemed delightfully familiar to its fashionable audience is progressively undermined.

In terms of act and scene structure, the play is tightly controlled. The roses of the opening, and the image of the country garden at the close, provide the natural framework for the two private, though formal, morning-room scenes of Act One and Act Four. At the centre stand juxtaposed the large-scale scenes: the ball, with band playing, banks of flowers and brilliant lights, in which the women are in the forefront; and the more sombre setting of Lord Darlington's rooms, the male preserve, where the latent hostility to women expressed in the brittle, heartless conversation of Dumby and Graham is reinforced by the contrast between their dark formal clothes and the isolation of the beautifully dressed Mrs Erlynne. It is social death not to be seen with a man at the first, and social infamy to be found with a man in the second. The visual dimension is as important in these comedies as in *Salomé*, and not just in terms of delight, though 'a play about society people by Oscar Wilde was inevitably a dress parade'. Lady Windermere's growth from innocence to maturity of judgment is partly conveyed by such contrasts as that between the opening image as she stands, her hands wet, to arrange the roses, and her exhaustion as she lies on the sofa at the beginning of Act Four; or when her refusal to shake hands with Lord Darlington in the opening sequence is recalled by the play's last gesture as she takes her husband's hand.

—Peter Raby, *Oscar Wilde* (Cambridge, England: Cambridge University Press, 1988): pp. 89–90.

☙

Patricia Flanagan Behrendt: The Subtext of Sexuality in Wilde's Dandies

[Patricia Flanagan Behrendt, assistant professor of theatre arts and dance at the University of Nebraska-Lincoln, is the author of *Oscar Wilde: Eros and Aesthetics* (1991). Behrendt reveals how Wilde's garden imagery underlies the sexual subtleties between Lord Darlington and Lady Winderemere.]

The play opens in the city with Lady Windermere, on her twenty-first birthday, engaged in the most superficial domestic task of arranging roses in a bowl. Wilde's use of city and country or garden motifs in his earlier work to contrast the intellectual with the instinctive respectively persists into the social comedies, where it illuminates the meaning behind certain otherwise simple settings. Since Wilde specifies that Lady Windermere is first seen arranging cut flowers, her prescribed activity is more significant than the traditional stage business of that type which is invented by the actor or the director. As the scene progresses we discover that the simple domestic task of flower arranging symbolizes her own naive notion that natural impulses or passions can be as easily managed as cut flowers. When Lord Darlington is announced, Lady Windermere's instincts govern her attempts to control the situation. She tells the butler to show Lord Darlington in, but then she adds "and I'm at home to any one who calls." Her subtext is that she does not want to be perceived as "at home" particularly or exclusively to Lord Darlington, who had annoyed her the previous evening by paying her "elaborate compliments."

When he enters, she uses the fact that her hands are wet from handling flowers to avoid physical contact with Lord Darlington. He then notices her fan, which she describes as a birthday present, with her name inscribed on it, from her husband. Since Darlington cannot take Lady Windermere's hand, he asks if he may examine the fan. In this scene Wilde plays upon the traditional idea that if one cannot touch the love object—in this case Lady Windermere—one touches something that belongs to the beloved. Since the fan is a gift from her husband, Lord Darlington's handling of it intimates that he is sexually intent upon intruding himself into their marital relationship.

Wilde specifies that Lady Windermere continues to arrange the roses while attempting to confront Lord Darlington with the fact that his flirtatious behavior annoys her. She is physically occupied with the roses which, as the classical symbols of passion or the antithesis of rationality, would seem to represent the nature of Darlington's regard for her. He, on the other hand, is occupied with her fan. Traditionally, the fan plays a significant role in flirtation scenes in which the female desires to attract the male, and it is therefore symbolically associated with female desire. However, in this scene Lady Windermere has not used the fan herself. Instead, Darlington has simply taken it up forcibly himself. And when one imagines the actor himself opening and closing the fan, in effect attempting to manipulate Lady Windermere's desire, the actual aggressiveness of Darlington's intentions becomes apparent. When he begins to manipulate Lady Windermere's thoughts and actions through the clever use of language, we see that his attentions are a form of assault, and his manipulation of her fan, in fact, a psychological assault, even a form of rape. One of the most overlooked aspects of dandy conversation is its inherent aggressiveness, in which the energy of libidinal desire is channeled into language.

The significance of Lord Darlington's arrival on Lady Windermere's twenty-first birthday is signalled by her announcement that she has just "come of age." The idea of coming of age generally refers to a legal rite of passage. However, the fact that Wilde does not elaborate on the legal or material nature of Lady Windermere's new status suggests that her announcement foreshadows a new phase in her development. The exact nature of that phase and its parallel in Christian myth become evident as Lady Windermere's character emerges in her conversation with Lord Darlington. The exchange between them, which explores the nature of "good and bad" and "right and wrong," reveals that Lady Windermere's unbending judgments are based entirely upon a total ignorance of real people and their motivations in real life. Despite the fact that Lady Windermere is married and has a six-month-old child, her malleability under Lord Darlington's influence implies that neither marriage nor child-bearing ensure any understanding of human experience. The contrast is an important one, for it signals the dichotomy with which the play is concerned: namely that certain socially accepted rites of passage have little to do with one's understanding of human experience and are false indicators of one's level of emotional and intellectual maturation.

Lady Windermere's objective in the opening scene is to chastise Lord Darlington for paying her what she believes to be false compliments. When he insists that he is sincere, she asserts that most men pay compliments that they don't mean and that he, on the other hand, is really "better than most men," and that he only "pretends to be worse." While attempting to sound as if she knows what most men are about, she reveals her own inexperience in discussing with such assured inaccuracy the complex motivations of Lord Darlington. In order further to ingratiate himself, Lord Darlington encourages her misperceptions by seeming to agree that "we all have our little vanities," implying that he desires merely to appear wicked. By encouraging Lady Windermere to feel that she is a perceptive woman of the world, Lord Darlington begins to maneuver her into an untenable position which will work to his advantage later. The two present a clear contract on stage between her vain assumptions about her own self-knowledge and his ambitious pandering to her which belies his superior intellect and his vast self-knowledge.

—Patricia Flanagan Behrendt, *Oscar Wilde: Eros and Aesthetics* (London, England: Macmillan Academic and Professional Ltd, 1991): pp. 128–131.

[Michael Patrick Gillespie is Louise Edna Goeden Professor
of English at Marquette University. His works include
Recent Criticism of James Joyce's Ulysses: *An Analytical
Review* (co-authored with Paula F. Gillespie), *Joyce Through
the Ages: A Nonlinear Approach, Oscar Wilde and the Poetics
of Ambiguity, Inverted Volumes Improperly Arranged: James
Joyce and His Trieste Library,* and *Reading the Book of Himself: Narrative Strategies in the Works of James Joyce.* Here,
Gillespie relates Wilde's famous performance on the opening
night of *Lady Winderemere's Fan.*]

This drive to develop his plays to a point just short of giving offense
to his Victorian audience proved to have an expansive rather than
inhibitive effect. One sees this especially in the way that it led Wilde
to augment the formal as well as contextual scope of each play. Both
his inclination toward brinkmanship and his desire to expand the
artistic parameters of drama are clearly demonstrated in Richard
Ellmann's account of the premiere of *Lady Windermere's Fan.*

In response to first-nighters' approval of his play, Wilde showed a
subtle awareness of the elastic boundaries of the medium in which
he worked. As he addressed the crowd in the theater, he extended the
performance that they were witnessing by creating yet another dramatic scene characterized by the both/and impulse of critiquing and
courting his audience.

> After the final curtain the applause was long and hearty,
> and Wilde came forward from the wings in response to
> cries of "Author!" He knew how he wished to look, and
> what he wanted to say. In his mauve-gloved hand was a
> cigarette . . . and in his buttonhole a green carnation. The
> "delightful and immortal speech" (as he himself described
> it in a letter to the *St. James's Gazette*) was accentuated,
> according to [actor and theater manager George]
> Alexander, in this way: "Ladies and gentlemen: I have
> enjoyed this evening *immensely.* The actors have given us a
> *charming* rendering of a *delightful* play, and your apprecia-
> tion has been *most* intelligent. I congratulate you on the
> *great* success of your performance, which persuades me
> that you think *almost* as highly of the play as I do myself."

As Ellmann's description implies, Wilde's performance had a calculated arrogance that stopped just short of the inflammatory gesture that would have compelled his listeners to oppose his audacity; but it also soothed sensitive feelings with an imbedded flattery, implying that only the most sophisticated could attend and appreciate such a play.

Another event at the premiere of *Lady Windermere's Fan* demonstrates Wilde's awareness of the value of not only prolonging the performance of the play beyond the last scene but also initiating the dramatic action before the first curtain actually rose. As Ellmann reports, Wilde arranged to have a number of his friends cause a stir by coming to the theater wearing green carnations similar to the one in his own buttonhole and to make an ostentatious display of taking their seats near the front. On the surface, the gesture seems innocuous; but, for a society already conditioned to follow with interest the subtle variances in Wilde's behavior, such an exquisite test of the limits of decorum (green carnations?) was bound to arouse interest. Because the flowers attracted attention as obvious signs without providing equally obvious indications of what they signified, the audience became engaged in creating meaning without feeling the need to follow the strictures of a prescribed response. Further, with the event itself acting as a kind of curtain raiser, it provided an implicit invitation to approach in the same manner the play that would follow.

—Michael Patrick Gillespie, *Oscar Wilde and the Poetics of Ambiguity* (Gainesville, Fla.: University Press of Florida, 1996): pp. 77–78.

ANNE VARTY: *LADY WINDERMERE'S FAN:* A PLAY ABOUT A GOOD WOMAN

[Anne Varty teaches at Royal Holloway University of London. Her main research interests are modern British and European Theatre and literature of the late Victorian period. She edited (with Robert Crawford) *Liz Lochhead's Voices* (Edinburgh UP, 1993) and is author of *A Preface to*

Oscar Wilde. She is currently editing an anthology of material from women's newspapers for the years' 1899–1901. In this excerpt, Varty traces the conflict between Wilde and his stage manager, George Alexander, regarding the plot of *Lady Windermere's Fan.*]

The play was first produced by George Alexander, the 34-year-old actor-manager at the St James's Theatre, London, on 20 February 1892 where it ran until 29 July before embarking on a provincial tour from 22 August to 29 October. It was immediately revived in London and ran from 31 October to 30 November. During this time it grossed a profit for Alexander's company of £5570.0.11, and Wilde, being paid a percentage of the box, earned £7000 from the play in its first year. His celebrity status was assured. *Lady Windermere's Fan* was published in 1893. The published version differs from the script that was performed on the first press night, although it is in line with the play that was performed within a week of its opening. The major alteration which Wilde effected early was to bring forward the revelation of Mrs Erlynne's identity as the mother of Lady Windermere. On the first night this information was withheld until the 'very end of the play'. Subsequently the audience became privy to this knowledge at the end of Act 2. Reviewing the first night, A. B. Walkley argued:

> If we were told at the outset, I, for one, should not view her conduct and Lord Windermere's in forcing her upon his wife with half the interest which these things afford me while still in the dark.
>
> (Critical Heritage)

This indeed was Wilde's thinking on the matter of delayed revelation, but already during rehearsals Alexander had been pressuring him to change the sequential release of information to the audience—and Wilde, at further advice from his friends, eventually gave in. ⟨. . .⟩

Wilde in fact lost nothing of his dual purpose which was to maintain the focus of interest on Mrs Erlynne and to avoid stereotype. The revision enhances the psychological complexity of the adventuress, and the audience is freed from atavistic curiosity about her identity. It is able to consider at greater leisure the exposure of immovable conventions of social etiquette, which would damn Mrs

Erlynne without reprieve, as artificial and corrupting in themselves. And it is able to see her as a 'type untouched by literature', by which Wilde meant more than simply the positive portrayal of an 'unmotherly mother': he constrcted Mrs Erlynne to fulfil his vision of the 'individualist', the ideal human type unique to Wilde's work, which dominates 'The Critic as Artist' and 'The Soul of Man Under Socialism'. As Wilde stated, 'Those who have seen *Lady Windermere's Fan* will see that if there is one particular doctrine contained in it, it is that of sheer individualism.'

The revised plot is as tightly constructed as a Platonic dialogue to interrogate assumed values and moral positions. Not least among these questioned absolutes are the notions, so dear to Ibsen, that sincerity, truth-telling and honesty are of paramount importance to the moral health of society. Three secrets are left at the end of the play, to which only the audience has access. All of them are in the gift of Mrs Erlynne. Lady Windermere never knows that Mrs Erlynne is her mother; Lord Windermere never hears about his wife's escapade with Lord Darlington; Lord Augustus is duped by Mrs Erlynne about what she was doing in Darlington's rooms. As Ellmann puts it, the play 'concludes with collusive concealment instead of collective disclosure. Society profits from deception.'

—Anne Varty, *A Preface to Oscar Wilde* (Essex, England: Addison Wesley Longman Limited, 1998): pp. 157–159.

☙

Neil Sammells: The Significance of a Fan

[Neil Cameron Sammells is the Dean of Humanities and Reader in English at Bath College of Higher Education, England. In addition to *Wilde Style: The Plays and Prose of Oscar Wilde* (2000), he has written *Tom Stoppard: The Artist as Critic,* and co-edited *Irish Writing: Exile and Subversion, Writing and Censorship in Britain,* and *Writing and America.* He is also author of numerous articles and reviews, and is the co-editor of *Irish Studies Review.* In this excerpt, Sammells traces the changing significance of *Lady Windermere's Fan* throughout the play.]

Lady Windermere's Fan was first produced on 20 February 1892 and enjoyed the longest run of Wilde's plays: 197 performances. Henry James rather sniffily noted its 'candid and primitive simplicity' and its 'perfectly reminiscential air.' Reminiscential it may be—of Sardou and Haddon Chambers's *The Idler* in particular, while Sydney Grundy accused Wilde of plagiarizing his own *The Glass of Fashion*—but primitive and candid it most certainly is not. At the beginning of the final act, with the play having come full circle to the Windermeres' morning room, we find Lady Windermere in an agony of self-recrimination and fear of discovery: has Mrs Erlynne come clean in Darlington's rooms and told the men of Lady Windermere's plan to leave her husband and child? 'Perhaps,' she soliloquizes, '[Mrs Erlynne] told them the true reason of her being there, and the real meaning of that—fatal fan of mine'. Lady Windermere, however does not know the 'true' reason (she never learns that Mrs Erlynne is her mother) and Wilde is at pains to prevent any 'real' meaning adhering to the fan as we follow its narrative trajectory, passed from hand to hand, through the play. The fan, the fashion accessory designed at once for display and concealment, floats free of fixed, authentic signification as it acquires shifting, multiple meanings in the course of the drama. It is an example of the way significant ephemera (Hebdige's safety-pin, pointed shoe, motorcycle and tube of vaseline) come to exercise a symbolic function, operating on 'the profoundly superficial level of appearances: that is, at the level of signs.' Despite Henry James, *Lady Windermere's Fan* has all the complexity of the fan itself. Indeed, the fan—which in the original production 'sported sixteen white ostrich feathers fixed to a handle of yellow tortoiseshell', and replicas of which, in a shrewd piece of merchandizing, audiences were told they could acquire from Duvelleroy's of Regent Street—signifies nothing so much as the nature of the play which bears its name. In short, the fan is subjected to that process of *bricolage* which defines Wilde's working methods in the Society Comedies.

Darlington notices the fan straight away in the opening moments, where it is offered as a token of the relationship between Lady Windermere and her husband: it carries her name and is a present for her twenty-first birthday, thus representing her coming of age and passage into experience. It connotes the domestic and the normative.

The first act ends with Lady Windermere promising to strike Mrs Erlynne with the fan if she dares to accept her husband's invitation to the ball: it now signifies her unbending puritanism and is a weapon of recrimination. During the neatly choreographed second act, the fan undergoes further transformations. It is handed to Darlington when Lady Windermere confronts her husband: 'A useful thing, a fan, isn't it? . . . I want a friend tonight, Lord Darlington; I didn't know I would want one so soon.' It thus signifies her shifting allegiances, and at the crucial moment when—in what she herself sees as an act of moral cowardice—Lady Windermere fails to strike Mrs Erlynne, she first clutches the fan then drops it to the floor. In Act 3, Cecil Graham spots the fan in Darlington's room and interprets it as an index of his hypocrisy: 'Darlington has been moralising and talking about the purity of love, and that sort of thing, and he has got some woman in his rooms all the time.' At this point in the play the fan also serves the conventional purpose of the 'significant' stage prop by bringing the action to the crisis of discovery: it signifies self-consciously the kind of play we are watching. At the act drop, Mrs Erlynne coolly picks up the fan and leaves—now it simultaneously signifies the self-cancelling confluence of deceit (Lady Windermere has slipped away and Mrs Erlynne allows herself to appear as Darlington's mistress) and self-sacrifice (Mrs Erlynne seems to have thrown away any chance of getting back into society and of snaring Lord Augustus). When, in Act Four, Mrs Erlynne comes back to return the fan, Lord Windermere sees it as a sign of her moral degeneracy: 'I can't bear the sight of it now. I shall never let my wife use it again. The thing is soiled for me. You should have kept it and not brought it back'. As the play moves towards its denouement the fan becomes a gift from Lady Windermere to Mrs. Erlynne.

It signifies both the latter's complicated motherly feelings (she continues to protect her daughter from painful knowledge), the daughter's new-won tolerance and sense of indebtedness, and further multiple concealments: Lady Windermere is keeping the truth from her husband, who is also keeping it from her. Finally, Lord Augustus is allowed to carry the fan—he has been instrumental in the deceit, and is now being duped into marriage by the 'clever' Mrs Erlynne. So, the fan is appropriated, displayed, passed on and variously transformed as a sign. By the end of the play its multiformity issues a direct challenge to the domestic normativity it connoted at the beginning. Indeed, it enjoys the same relationship to that normativity as the Mod's business-suit does to the world of the city banker.

The fan, of course, is a literal example of the stylish object: it is a desirable commodity which connects directly with the fashionable world of the audience, but which acquires new and everchanging significances according to the way it is appropriated and displayed. The fluidity of meaning which Wilde ascribes to the fan is matched by the indeterminacy of his principal characters. They are opened out, displayed, snapped shut, one surface reversed flamboyantly to reveal another. Lady Windermere is at once the uncompromising puritan and the obverse: a sort of aristocratic Nora Helmer prepared to leave her husband and child. The opening scene brings her into contact with the dandy Lord Darlington who begins as a predatory opportunist (he and the Duchess of Berwick circle Lady Windermere like social sharks), acts as the spokesperson of a high-octane individualism when he tries to persuade Lady Windermere to run off with him ('You said once you would make no compromise with things. Make none now. Be brave! Be yourself!') and who disappears from the play as a confirmed and heart-broken sentimentalist. Lord Windermere begins as surrogate-father and protector, warning his wife against judging Mrs Erlynne too hastily, and in the final act adopts the rhetoric of puritanism in his condemnation of the 'worthless, vicious' Mrs Erlynne after she is found in Darlington's rooms (he cannot contain his horror at this 'divorced woman going about under an assumed name' and it is hard not to feel this is a bathetic example of self-consciously Wildean rhetorical overlay). Mrs Erlynne—the female dandy who displaces both Darlington and Lord Windermere as the locus of 'male' wit and control—is the amoral adventuress, the 'woman with a past' who 'wins all' at the end. She is also the mouthpiece for a social and emotional conventionalism when, in Act 3, she tries to persuade her daughter to return to her doll's house: 'if [Lord Windermere] was harsh to you, you must stay with your child. If he ill-treated you, you must stay with your child. If he abandoned you your place is with your child.' This is not a case of Wilde revealing hidden psychological depths beneath surface appearances, but rather of his creating *dramatis personae* defined by verbal and theatrical styles, which cancel each other out. As Mrs Erlynne says, 'there is a great deal of good in Lord Augustus. Fortunately it is all on the surface. Just where good qualities should be.' Her remark neatly collapses that distinction between surface and depth which so much analysis of the play is predicated upon. Part of what defines the stylization at work in the play is the rapidity and emphatic theatricality with which the characters swap one posture, one surface, one signification for another. This is characterization as *bricolage,* and it is entirely consistent with Wilde's theoretical assertion that language is the parent and not the child of thought. Styled by language and literary form, his characters are dramatic examples of the post-structuralist subject, dispersed and decentered by the processes of signification which simultaneously bring it into being.

—Neil Sammells, *Wilde Style: The Plays and Prose of Oscar Wilde* (England: Pearson Education Limited, 2000): pp. 85–88.

Plot Summary of
A Woman of No Importance

Among Oscar Wilde's four social comedies, *A Woman of No Importance* is distinct in its dramatic structure in that the so-called secondary characters of the play take on much larger roles in the dialogue than in any of the other three plays. Lady Caroline, Lady Hunstanton, Lady Stutfield, Mrs. Allonby—with the additions of Sir John and Mr. Kelvil—dominate the first act and most of the second act, whereas the title character, Mrs. Arbuthnot, does not even make an appearance until the second half of the second act. In the other three plays, *Lady Windermere's Fan, The Importance of Being Earnest,* and *The Ideal Husband,* the main characters—either a duo or trio—are solidly represented from the very opening of the play. In *A Woman of No Importance,* Lord Illingworth is the first of the main characters with whom we make proper acquaintance. We are prepared to like him, as he is Wilde's specialty—certified dandy—but in Lord Illingworth there is little of Algernon's talent for mock mockery or Darlington's romantic pathos. We are not meant to take Lady Stutfield seriously in anything she says, but Wilde is not being entirely flirtatious when he gives her the line: "Every one *I* know says you are very, very wicked."

Wicked or not, Illingworth is absolutely selfish. When Lady Hunstanton compliments his kindness in hiring the conscientious but nameless Gerald Arbuthnot as his personal secretary, he remarks that there is nothing of kindness in his choice, but that his employment of the young man occurred purely for the sake of convenience. In fact, Lord Illingworth's appeal to his companions lies in his constant stream of aphorisms, which are clearly intelligent but also dangerously cynical such that those around him have no choice but to be intimidated into accepting his outrageous utterances lest they themselves suffer the attention of his sharp tongue. In a political debate with Mr. Kelvil, Illingworth produces his central doctrine: "One should never take sides in anything, Mr. Kelvil. Taking sides is the beginning of sincerity, and earnestness follows shortly afterwards, and the human being becomes a bore." Clearly, Lord Illingworth, one of the most eligible, but also most elusive, bachelors in London, does not lack in interest. If purging oneself of sincerity and earnestness is the price for such social eminence, Lord Illingworth has gladly paid his dues.

In the opening scene of *Lady Windermere's Fan,* Lord Darlington tells Lady Windermere that anything is better than being sacrificed. Based on his actions, it seems that Lord Illingworth would not agree. In his youth, he fathered a son whom he subsequently refused to recognize as his own and whose mother he refused to marry. Having willingly lost contact with both mother and child for two decades, Lord Illingworth finds himself face to face with the woman whom he has ruined when he is introduced to Gerald's mother. She has become an entirely different creature from the naïve and trusting girl she was before her great disappointment. Deeply embittered and obsessively maternal, she forbids her son from accepting the position with the wealthy ambassador, whom she feels does not deserve the admiration of her son, even while fearing that he will contaminate Gerald with his dark eloquence.

Gerald cannot know why his mother dislikes his new employer, and determines, with the advice of Lord Illingworth, that his new position is merely the necessary separation between mother and son. She, thrown into desperate turmoil at the unexpected intrusion of this loathed man, cannot but appear terribly unreasonable in her pleas to Gerald that he refuse the most promising opportunity of his lifetime, and he is harsh in his denouncement of her: "You have always tried to crush my ambition, mother—haven't you? You have told me that the world is a wicked place, that success is not worth having, that society is shallow, and all that sort of thing—well, I don't believe it, mother. I think the world must be delightful. I think society must be exquisite. I think success is a thing worth having. You have been wrong in all that you have taught me, mother, quite wrong."

Youth and ignorance are the cruelest judges. Mrs. Arbuthnot was her son's age when she determined that she must suffer, both for her failed love for Illingworth and for the product of that love, her son. This insistence for over-determination resonates with the earlier introduction of the young American heiress, Miss Hester Worsley, who outspokenly formulates her own version of doom-eager morality: "Let all women who have sinned be punished. . . . It is right that they should be punished, but don't let them be the only ones to suffer. If a man and woman have sinned, let them both go forth into the desert to love or loathe each other there. Let them both be branded. Set a mark, if you wish, on each, but don't punish the one and let the other go free. Don't have one law for men and another for women." Hester's egalitarian condemnation of sin falls on deaf ears in the party at the English country house; it is made less relevant than Lady Caroline's needlework or Lady Hunstanton's observation of her supposed prettiness in giving the speech. Still, in spite of Hester's apparent irrelevance to the English ladies around her, such hardness is a startling statement from someone so young and without experience of evil, which only gives emphasis to the fact that the little American is decisively not of Wilde's world.

What, then, is Hester's dramatic function? She forms the crucial third leg that sustains the otherwise hopelessly unbalanced formation created by Gerald's naïve hopes and his mother's secret neurosis. Yet the Hester of the play's first act cannot help Mrs. Arbuthnot. Ironically, it may have been Lord Illingworth who causes the necessary shift in Hester's previously flawed vision. Acting on an experiment suggested by Mrs. Allonby regarding the nature of women, Lord Illingworth attempts to prove that all women are flattered by men who make love to them by kissing Hester, who, much to his surprise, flees him in real terror. The experience does not damage Hester, but rather shows her the possibility for anyone—even herself—to acquire moral stain by the caprice of others. She recants her belief that God's law requires that sinners, and their children, be punished for their misfortunes, and becomes Mrs. Arbuthnot's partner in suffering, if not in punishment.

The play reaches its climax at **the end of the third act** in which Mrs. Arbuthnot tries to reveal to her son Lord Illingworth's true nature by relating a hypothetical story of "a girl once" who fell in love with the man but was cruelly abandoned by him. She resigns her effort when he responds to her tale with as little compassion as his beloved Hester: "My dear mother, it all sounds very tragic, of course. But I dare say the girl was just as much to blame as Lord Illingworth was.—After all, would a really nice girl, a girl with any nice feelings at all, go away from her home with a man to whom she was not married, and live with him as his wife? No nice girl would." Just a few moments after he utters these words, Hester rushes into the room screaming for rescue from the man who has insulted her, and Gerald indeed jumps to her rescue and vows that he will kill the villain. The act drops on the frantic mother who, unable to physically hold back her son from harming Illingworth, finally cries out: "Stop, Gerald, stop! He is your own father!"

The knowledge of his mother's shame does not seem to teach Gerald very much at all, for his next action after rejecting his father's offer for employment is to demand that his mother restore her good name and marry Illingworth at once. Mrs. Arbuthnot, as willing as she is to sacrifice her love for Gerald for the sake of his happiness, is absolutely firm in her refusal to sacrifice her hatred for Illingworth for anyone's sake. Even when Illingworth himself appears at her door, claiming paternal love for the boy and proposing marriage to gain his son, Mrs. Arbuthnot calmly declines and turns him out of the door. There is no room in her heart for any new loves save her son and his betrothed, who spreads moral and financial security over them all. ❁

List of Characters in
A Woman of No Importance

Lord Illingworth: The most eligible bachelor in London, who habitually proclaims sweeping aphorisms concerning the human condition, which seem to hold up only when one does not think very long, or at all, upon them. He appoints Gerald Arbuthnot as his secretary, only to find that the young man is actually his son, the child of the woman he refused to marry two decades ago. Lord Illingworth is no less arrogant or irresponsible than he was in his youth, and despite his stated interest and affection for his newly recovered son, he remains smugly insensitive to the distress of both mother and son, emphasizing only the potential of his position for Gerald.

Gerald Arbuthnot: Gerald is even more naïve than he is young. He idolizes Lord Illingworth, who has offered him his path of fortune and social prominence. Seduced by the prospect of wealth, Gerald Arbuthnot seems ready to abandon his mother in favor of Illingworth, for he cannot understand why she does not give him her blessings for his new position. When he discovers the true identity of his new employer and the disgrace he has caused his mother and himself, Gerald demands that justice and duty be upheld, that Illingworth marry his mother and raise her from her shame despite her insistence that she will not join herself in marriage to the man she has hated with her whole being for twenty years.

Mrs. Arbuthnot: Rachel Arbuthnot's adult identity relies on her past as the wronged and fallen woman. She has embraced this role so completely that she is unwilling to give it up, even at the desperate pleas of her son. Having abandoned hope for personal happiness as a mere twenty-year-old, Mrs. Arbuthnot is all maternal instinct. For two decades, her only comfort has been the self-inflicted punishment of rigid morality and the knowledge that what she calls her dishonor is inseparable from her love for her son, which she holds sacred. Gerald's mother can only accept herself if she can retain her identity as the sacrificed and sacrificing mother.

Miss Hester Worsley: A young American Puritan, Miss Worsley is extremely opinionated in her moral and religious beliefs. Equally unwavering in her American optimism and provincial rigidity, Hester outspokenly disapproves of English Society. Miss Worsley is an orphan and wealthy heiress. She falls in love with Gerald Arbuthnot, and subsequently saves him from moral compromise by bringing to him herself as well as her wealth, in marriage. At the play's start, Miss Worsley lectures the other ladies at the English country house that men and women who have sinned must, without exception, endure due punishment, but her love for Gerald and his fallen mother convince her, by the play's end, that "God's law is only Love."

Mrs. Allonby: An extremely shrewd woman whose scruples are somewhat less commendable than her wit, Mrs. Allonby sportingly commissions Lord Illingworth to kiss "the Puritan," Miss Worsley. Mrs. Allonby is outspoken about her conception of the "ideal husband," which is self-consciously egotistical if not coyly cynical.

Lady Hunstanton: Lady Hunstanton provides the country house at which the acts of the play take place. She is a constant gossip who, paradoxically, is always confused about the particular details of her stories. Jane Hunstanton's great fault, according to Lady Caroline, is that she dimly believes good of everyone.

Sir John Pontefract: Sir John may very well be the most resigned man in London. His efforts to assert himself over his overbearing wife are never successful, and even his tentative attempt to raise an impotent flirtation with the obliging Lady Stutfield is systematically thwarted by the ever-alert Lady Caroline.

Lady Caroline Pontefract: Lady Caroline's dramatically identifying trait is her need to constantly nag her mild-mannered husband, Sir John. Shamelessly self-contradictory, Lady Caroline provides a constant stream of idiosyncratic social commentary, which is sometimes even true in spite of herself. Despite her pathetic displays over her husband, Lady Caroline is an extremely sharp woman, who is, in fact, rather too sharp for her sluggishly complacent husband.

Mr. Kelvil, M.P.: Mr. Kelvil is a comically long-suffering man of the state, who delights in despairing of the downfall of national morality. When asked by Lady Stutfield what he has been lately writing about, he replies with great self-satisfaction, "On the usual subject. On Purity."

Lady Stutfield: Lady Stutfield is Society's professionally insipid yes-woman, who has a habit of repeating most adjectives she utters twice. She seems to hang upon every word that falls from anyone's lips, and especially those of Mrs. Allonby when she discourses upon the attributes of the Ideal Man. ❀

Critical Views on
A Woman of No Importance

Epifanio San Juan Jr.: Change and Stasis in
Wilde's Women

[Epifanio San Juan Jr. is professor and chair of the Depart-
ment of Comparative American Cultures at Washington
State University. He has also taught at the University of Cal-
ifornia, University of Connecticut, Brooklyn College of
CUNY, and Tamkang University, Taiwan. His books include
*The Art of Oscar Wilde, Beyond Postcolonial Theory, From
Exile to Diaspora, After Postcolonialism,* and *The Racial
Imaginary,* due out in 2001. This excerpt focuses on the ver-
bose and melodramatic characters of Hester Worsley and
Mrs. Arbuthnot in *A Woman of No Importance.*]

Wilde's fertile inventiveness provides a mode of fulfilling his impulse
for exhibitionism, for the ostentatious show of his virtuosity. A
variety of texture and tone in speech results. Hester's flamboyance
and pompous solemnity contrasts with the pithy epigrams of Lord
Illingworth (e.g., "Nothing succeeds like excess"). The dry, elegant
aphorisms of Wilde's dandies seem to infect the conversation of the
other characters in the comedies. In the case of Lord Illingworth, his
engaging wit redeems his callousness, his coarseness and vulgarity.
On the other hand, there is something distasteful in Hester's stern
pronouncements, which make her into an unlikely sage of eighteen.
Mrs. Arbuthnot, like Hester, has a flair for flatulent oratory; she
tends to convert pathos into a sticky fudge of verbiage. In between the
thunderous curtains we listen to the pedestrian drivel of "the mindless
boors" and "sycophantic cronies." A typical verbal trick of substitution
occurs in the mannerisms of some of the "flat" characters, in Dr.
Daubeny's repetitions, or in Lady Hunstanton's forgetfulness: "I was in
hopes he would have married Lady Kelso. But I believe he said her
family was too large. Or was it her feet?" Saying that Lady Belton had
eloped with Lord Fethersdale, she adds, "Poor Lord Belton died three
days afterwards of joy, or gout. I forget which. . . ."

After Hester has observed and heard Mrs. Arbuthnot, she relaxes
her obstinate casuistry a bit, confessing to her future mother-in-law:

"When you came into the drawingroom this evening, somehow you brought with you a sense of what is good and pure in life. I had been foolish. There are things that are right to say, but that may be said at the wrong time and to the wrong people." But though she may adjust herself to the situation, her corresponding attitudes remain fixed: "It is right that the sins of the parents should be visited on the children." Later she amends this "just" law. After Lord Illingworth's attempt to kiss her, and in her sympathy with the anguished Mrs. Arbuthnot, Hester now believes that "God's law is only Love."

Such a change in thinking springs from Hester's emotional susceptibility: she is either totally angry or totally sympathetic. Her moods and affections easily influence her judgments. Mrs. Arbuthnot, unlike Hester, alters her decisions in consonance with her attachment to her past. Reminded by her son, in Act II, that she is also in part guilty of her youthful "indiscretion," she yields to Gerald's wish; in Act III, however, she reverses her decision. While Gerald seeks to reconcile his parents in marriage, his mother, in righteous indignation, elects a double standard and affirms the inequality of fate between men and women: "It is the usual history of a man and a woman, as it usually happens, as it always happens. And the ending is the ordinary ending. The woman suffers. The man goes free." This view prevents her from allowing for the imperfections of men and the absurdities of experience. Her judgments run on one track, permitting no possibility of growth or improvement in the process of life. She denies the possibility of an inward change in the character of Lord Illingworth: "It is not what Lord Illingworth believes, or what he does not believe, that makes him bad. It is what he is." The recollection of the past seems to reduce her sensibility into a stasis of empty despair, which she rationalizes by her lachrymose portrayals of her suffering as a martyr of womankind. She is almost redundant in her reactions, which one can easily predict. In short, she can easily be "typed":

> GERALD. Is it fair to go back twenty years in any man's career? And what have you or I to do with Lord Illingworth's early life? What business is it of ours?
>
> MRS. ARBUTHNOT. What this man has been, he is now, and will be always.

Evidently she is trying to liken him to herself in her stubborn clinging to her guilty past. Consequently she thinks of her "sin" as being visited on her innocent child. Nothing has changed for her in twenty years; one can even say that she has indulged in her role as victim. Whereas to Lord Illingworth "what is over is over," to Mrs. Arbuthnot the past lives on as a perpetual curse hovering in the air wherever she goes.

—Epifanio San Juan Jr., *The Art of Oscar Wilde* (Princeton, N.J.: Princeton University Press, 1967): pp. 160–163.

Christopher S. Nassaar: Daughters of Herodias

[Christopher S. Nassaar is Associate Professor of English at the American University of Beirut, is the author of *Into the Demon Universe: A Literary Exploration of Oscar Wilde* (1974) and *Oscar Wilde:* The Importance of Being Earnest, a study guide reprinted annually. He recently completed three further studies on influences on Wilde. In this excerpt, Nassaar's analysis of Wilde's garden imagery in *A Woman of No Importance* finds strong incestuous undertones between Mrs. Arbuthnot and Gerald.]

The garden imagery of *A Woman of No Importance* is a crucial key to the play's meaning. "The Book of Life begins with a man and a woman in a garden," Lord Illingworth observes in act 1, and Mrs. Allonby replies that "it ends with Revelations." Illingworth's affair with Mrs. Allonby had begun in her father's garden, and in act 1 Mrs. Allonby begins a tentative affair with him in a garden. Gardens and flowers are associated in the play with lust and sin. Mrs. Allonby, in act 1, wishes to walk to the conservatory because "Lord Illingworth told me this morning that there was an orchid there as beautiful as the seven deadly sins." Given these previous associations, it is disturbing when Mrs. Arbuthnot uses garden imagery when referring to her son in act 2:

MRS. ARBUTHNOT. George, don't take my son away from me. I have had twenty years of sorrow, and I have only had one thing to love me, only one thing to love. You have had a life of joy, and pleasure, and success. You have been quite happy,

you have never thought of us. There was no reason,
according to your views of life, why you should have
remembered us at all. Your meeting us was a mere accident, a horrible accident. Forget it. Don't come now, and
rob me of . . . of all I have in the whole world. You are so
rich in other things. Leave me the little vineyard of my life;
leave me the walled-in garden and the well of water; the
ewe-lamb God sent me, in pity or in wrath, oh! leave me
that. George, don't take Gerald from me.

[Woman]

Gerald is compared to a vineyard and a walled-in garden. A faint fragrance of incest begins to fill the air, but the odor remains very faint
at this point. ⟨. . .⟩

Act 4 is the most interesting act of the play, for in it Mrs.
Arbuthnot shows herself—to the perceptive reader or viewer—as a
true daughter of Herodias, a cultured Victorian version of Salome.
In this act, she reveals the true reasons why she abandoned Illingworth as soon as their child was born. One reason is that the child
displaced the father as the object of her affection and she wanted
him entirely for herself: she took the male child for her lover and ran
away with him. In a gush of emotion, Mrs. Arbuthnot explains
herself to Gerald:

MRS. ARBUTHNOT. No office is too mean, no care too lowly for the
thing we women love—and oh! How *I* loved *you*. Not
Hannah, Samuel more. And you needed love, for you
were weakly, and only love could have kept you alive.
Only love can keep any one alive. . . .
   You thought I spent too much of my time in going to
Church, and in Church duties. But where else could I
turn? God's house is the only house where sinners are
made welcome, and you were always in my heart, Gerald,
too much in my heart. For, though day after day, at morn
or evensong, I have knelt in God's house, I have never
repented of my sin. How could I repent of my sin when
you, my love, were its fruit! Even now that you are bitter
to me I cannot repent. I do not. You are more to me than
innocence. I would rather be your mother—oh! much
rather!—than have always been pure. . . . Oh, don't you
see? don't you understand?

[Woman]

The fruit of Mrs. Arbuthnot's adventure in her father's garden was Gerald, and she has been feasting on that fruit ever since. The fragrance of incest is no longer faint but very strong. Mrs. Arbuthnot's name—Rachel—also indicates her incestuous character, for the biblical Rachel was both Jacob's cousin and, along with her sister Leah, his wife. Jacob, moreover, was a younger brother who cheated his elder brother Esau of the rights and privileges of seniority. Wilde is very clever, though, for it is possible to see Mrs. Arbuthnot as a sentimental, tender-hearted mother. The mask is lifted only for the very perceptive. Mrs. Arbuthnot herself seems quite blind to her incestuous feelings. She has placed upon her eyes, not the covering of him who would see his God, but simply the covering of excessive sentimentality.

Ironically, Hester overhears Mrs. Arbuthnot, rushes to her, and embraces her. Hester had earlier declared that a man and a woman who have sinned should both be punished, but now she rejects her harsh Puritan attitude and insists that God's law is love. What she means, though, is that God's law is love for Gerald, since she shows no inclination whatsoever to forgive Lord Illingworth. The reason she forgives Mrs. Arbuthnot is because she recognizes a deep kinship with her: "In her all womanhood is martyred. Not she alone, but all of us are stricken in her house." Gerald had been insisting that his mother and Lord Illingworth marry, if only formally, for duty's sake.

Marriage, however, places the male in a dominant position, and what both Hester and Mrs. Arbuthnot seem to want is the opposite of this. In the parent-child relationship, the parent controls the child, and this is one reason Mrs. Arbuthnot had preferred Gerald to Illingworth. "You were weakly," she says to her son. Gerald, it seems, is destined to remain controlled. When he approaches Hester, she waves him back for having dared to insist that his mother marry Illingworth: "You cannot love me at all, unless you love her also. You cannot honour me, unless she's holier to you." The result is that Gerald withdraws his request, kneels before his mother, kisses her hands, and says: "You are my mother and my father all in one. I need no second parent."

It is only after Gerald has been literally brought to his knees that the two women are satisfied. Hester, moreover, has identified herself so thoroughly with Mrs. Arbuthnot that the latter now considers her an appropriate wife for Gerald:

MRS. ARBUTHNOT. (*Rises, and taking Hester by the hand, goes slowly over to where Gerald is lying on the sofa with his head buried*

> *in his hands. She touches him and he looks up.*) Gerald, I
> cannot give you a father, but I have brought you a wife.
> GERALD. Mother, I am not worthy either of her or you.
> MRS. ARBUTHNOT. So she comes first, you are worthy. And when
> you are away, Gerald . . . with . . . her—oh, think of me
> sometimes. Don't forget me.
>
> [*Woman*]

Mrs. Arbuthnot had said earlier that she could not repent of her sin, and she does not repent now. She brings Gerald a girl in her own image and practically instructs the boy to think of his mother when he is making love to his wife. Vicariously, Mrs. Arbuthnot will remain Gerald's lover.

This incestuous marriage is given a final dramatic twist at the end of the play. Gerald and Hester are in the garden together, but the mother does not follow them, so they return to fetch her. Gerald kneels down besides his mother:

> MRS. ARBUTHNOT. My boy! My boy! My boy! (*Running her fingers
> through his hair.*)
> HESTER. (*Coming over.*) But you have two children now. You'll let
> me be your daughter?
> MRS. ARBUTHNOT (*Looking up.*) Would you choose me for a
> mother?
> HESTER. You of all women I have ever known.
>
> [*Woman*]

To the Victorians, this must have been a charming and tender scene. What has happened, though, is that Hester, by embracing Mrs. Arbuthnot as her mother, has symbolically made herself Gerald's sister. Her marriage to Gerald, then, is the marriage of a brother and sister.

It is marriage, moreover, that will be dominated by Rachel Arbuthnot, who seems an inseparable part of it. Like the biblical Jacob, Gerald will have two wives, both incestuously related to him. Appropriately, the play ends with the three, intertwined like a spider web, withdrawing into the ubiquitous garden, the symbol of lust and sin. Mrs. Arbuthnot began her adult life in her father's garden with Lord Illingworth. Spiritually, she has never developed beyond that garden. Human nature being what it is, all human beings—Puritans included—enter the garden of Eros as soon as they emerge from the shell of innocence, and they remain there the rest of their lives. Mrs.

Arbuthnot is a woman of no importance because she is like every-body else in this respect.

—Christopher S. Nassaar, *Into the Demon Universe: A Literary Explo-ration of Oscar Wilde* (New Haven, Conn.: Yale University Press, 1974): pp. 113–119.

(ॐ)

Alan Bird: Women of Importance in *A Woman of No Importance*

[Alan Bird is the author of *The Plays of Oscar Wilde* (1977). In this selection, Bird discusses Wilde's compro-mise between plot and character development in *A Woman of No Importance*.]

An initial weakness of construction is that whilst there are reversals of attitude there are none of any importance in the plot; and such as there are of both varieties are concentrated in the last act. Normally, a dramatist seeks to introduce a new character, frequently with a dif-ferent attitude or viewpoint, later in the play so as to provide variety and contrast or a fresh development in the plot. Hester, the Amer-ican heiress, would have been the ideal candidate for this task but Wilde's anxiety to make his social attitudes clear from the beginning of the play obliges him to introduce her early in Act I, and thus he denies sufficient interest to the succeeding acts. Yet another weakness arises from the scene at the end of Act I when Lord Illingworth and Mrs. Allonby chat together about the attitudes of men and women towards each other: the conversation turns into a duel of wits from which Mrs. Allonby emerges undefeated—which, perhaps, implies that Mrs. Arbuthnot's yielding to Lord Illingworth years ago was as much the consequences of her own emotional nature and her own desires as the importunities of Lord Illingworth. But it is apparent to the audience that Lord Illingworth and Mrs. Allonby are actually flirting with each other and that there is a clear degree of sexual attraction between them: since Wilde does not exploit this further he has only managed to set the audience off on a false trail which is not directly relevant to the action although it does emphasise the moral ambivalences of a society which is prompt to condemn a 'sinner' like

Mrs. Arbuthnot whilst ignoring equally culpable behaviour provided it is discreetly conducted and not brought out into the open. Hunstanton Chase is to be seen as representative of superficial moral respectability whilst Mrs. Arbuthnot's home at Wrockley seems quite sure in its attitudes despite its being a house of 'sin'. ⟨. . .⟩

Mrs. Arbuthnot has, in fact, been driven to search deep into her own inner feelings: she now realises, for the first time, that her life has been based on a falsehood, that far from wishing the father of her child to marry her she wishes nothing of the sort. Her purpose in life is motherhood unadulterated by marriage. In this sense Mrs. Arbuthnot's stance is close to that taken up by the suffragettes and, still further on in the century, by the various women's liberation movements: for the late eighteen-nineties her views were revolutionary although obscured by the use of such words as 'sin', 'the mire of my life', 'sinner', and so on. It can be argued that Mrs. Arbuthnot, like Mrs. Erlynne (and Mrs. Cheveley in *An Ideal Husband* and all the women in *The Importance of Being Earnest*), is a study in female obsessiveness, all of them linked, perhaps, with the outsize personality of his mother Speranza. In Wilde's plays, generally, the men are impotent triflers, the women domineering, powerful, ruthless, self-possessed and absolutely determined in their obsessive desires and loves, whether of money, marriage, social standing, or a son.

> —Alan Bird, *The Plays of Oscar Wilde* (London, England: Vision Press Limited, 1977): pp. 120–121, 127–128.

⟨ℬ⟩

RODNEY SHEWAN: *A WOMAN OF NO IMPORTANCE:*
A NEO-RESTORATION CONFLICT

[Rodney Shewan is the author of *Oscar Wilde: Art and Egotism* (1977). In this excerpt, Shewan contrasts the values of the dandy and the puritan in Wilde's treatment of *A Woman of No Importance*.]

These attitudes, dramatically and morally critical of the libertine tradition, confirm the significance of Wilde's description of this as 'a woman's play'. The dandy's standards may carry the first two acts, but the puritans' standards carry the last two and determine the outcome of the plot. In spite of the varied and amusing social commentary of Act I and the dandy's catechism in Act III, it is 'the woman question' which predominates. Even Illingworth concedes to Gerald that women rule society. Even the female dandy, Mrs Allonby, verbally glittering amongst the dowagers and coffee-cups after dinner, builds a psychological maquette of the Ideal Man pinched into changing shapes wholly at the whim of the female ego. Even Lady Stutfield, who knows so few adverbs that she always uses them in pairs to compensate, can perceive a woman's advantages as Mrs Allonby assesses them: 'We have a much better time than they have. There are far more things forbidden to us than are forbidden to them'. Even Hester, who first declared that 'a woman who has sinned should never be forgiven', comes to recognize Mrs Arbuthnot as a figure in whom 'all womanhood is martyred', and sides with her against the common enemy.

The play resolves itself into a crude battle of sex between Hester and Mrs Allonby on the one hand and Lord Illingworth on the other, the booty being Gerald. Illingworth's parting vulgarism and Mrs Arbuthnot's retort to it define the antagonism succinctly. Rebuffed and chagrined, Illingworth assumes the manner of the professional rake: 'It's been an amusing experience to have met amongst people of one's own rank, and treated quite seriously too, one's mistress and one's –'; but he is cut short by a duellist's device: a glove (one of his own) slapped across his face. At the real moment of crisis, the woman meets the man of his own terms. ⟨. . .⟩

It is also a deliberate echo of the exchange between Illingworth and Mrs Allonby in Act I, in which Mrs Allonby had suggested that, if Illingworth tried to kiss Hester, she would 'Either marry you, or strike you across the face with her glove. What would you do if she stuck you across the face with her glove?' 'Fall in love with her, probably', replies Illingworth.

Although the women win the tug-of-war for Gerald, Wilde clearly has little sympathy with their position. To many of the audience, the vanquishing of the dandy or pseudo-libertine must have seemed like moral justice. To the dramatist it can only have seemed, depressingly, like more than usually accurate social realism. Illingworth admires the 'beautiful, passionate letter' written by Gerald to convince him to marry Mrs Arbuthnot at last, but adds, 'no son of mine should side with the Puritans: that is an error'. Indeed, Wilde went some way towards making the play explicitly anti-puritan after the best libertine tradition, but was obliged by Beerbohm Tree to cut his biggest libertine speech, presumably for fear of audience reaction. Sufficient comment remained, even so, to make his intellectual position clear, for the puritan–dandy antagonism is expressed at every level. The orchid, 'as beautiful as the seven deadly sins', that Mrs Allonby goes to look for in the Hunstanton conservatory in Act I, is contrasted with Mrs Arbuthnot's sitting-room, visited by Lady Hunstanton and Mrs Allonby in Act IV, 'the room of a sweet saint' with 'fresh natural flowers' and 'books that don't shock one'. The female dandy's set piece on the Ideal Man is pointedly juxtaposed with Hester's jeremiad on English society, especially on Lord Weston, Lady Caroline's brother, Lady Hunstanton is 'afraid that some of this clever talk may have shocked' Hester, but Mrs Allonby replies, 'Ah, that will do her so much good!'. ⟨. . .⟩

The central scenes of the play, those between Illingworth and Gerald, and Illingworth and Mrs Arbuthnot, are studies in lack of communication. This dismissal is the first and only instance of 'genuine communication' between the rival parties. The well-intentioned scheme of the cultural orphan, Gerald, for uniting his disparate parents is intrinsically absurd, mere lip-service to the social conventions which, for differing reasons, they both despise. Instead, Gerald himself marries, rejecting the dandy's values and espousing those of the American puritan, who also happens to be literally an orphan, and to posses a large fortune. The two orphans and the natural mother retire to 'other countries over sea, better, wiser, and less unjust'. Mrs Arbuthnot exchanges a tainted pastoral—the 'little walled-in garden' of her love for Gerald—for the wide open spaces of the democracy where suffering is given its due. As in *Lady Windermere's Fan,* the puritans recoup their vital forces in the 'country'. As in *The Way of the World,* one might also remark, it is the passionate dupe, or her Wildean equivalents, whose last resort takes the form of pastoral retreat. 'Well, friend,' says the pathetic Lady Wishfort to the delinquent Marwoud, 'you are enough to reconcile me to the bad world, or else I would retire to desarts and solitudes; and feed harmless sheep by groves and purling streams. Dear Marwoud, let us leave the world, and retire by ourselves and be shepherdesses.' The comic parallel is pertinent, for, from the dandy-libertine's viewpoint, the Arbuthnots' progression from Wrokley to America amounts to little more than exchanging a rabbit-hutch for a paddock. It may not be comic, but it ought to be laughable. As far as personal development is concerned, they might as well be dead. But in the interests of complete poetic justice, and completer comic peripeteia, Wilde lets Mrs Arbuthnot imply what we already suspect—that for her, Illingworth might equally as well be dead. It is implication rather than statement, for the last line of the play supports more weight, perhaps, that it is really built to bear. Is it the sign of Mrs Arbuthnot's long-awaited emancipation from her past, or is it merely dismissive revenge? Is she finally free of Illingworth's baneful tyranny over her imagination, or is she simply pleased to turn the tables on him, so reinforcing her self-destructive bitterness? Wilde leaves the epigram to its own devices, but the ending remains consistent with his ruling comic principle. Illingworth quits the scene, defeated and insulted, not as a result of anyone's moral denunciation but as a direct result of his own spontaneous vulgarity. 'Manners before morals' indeed. Those who exploit social gestures for their own ends must expect to be judged by them. Wilde's second pseudo-libertine, like his first, is dismissed from the critical commonweal not for interfering with the puritan's standards but for compromising his own.

—Rodney Shewan, *Oscar Wilde: Art and Egotism* (London, England: The Macmillan Press Ltd, 1977): pp. 169–170, 176–177.

⊛

SOS ELTIS: STAGING THE VILLAIN AND THE HEROINE IN *A WOMAN OF NO IMPORTANCE*

[Sos Eltis has taught at St. John's College, Oxford, and Boston University. He is currently a Fellow in English at Brasenose College, Oxford. In this excerpt, Eltis emphasizes the power struggle between Lord Illingworth and Mrs. Arbuthnot.]

Wilde's final version of Lord Illingworth is neither a melodramatic villain nor a romanticized wicked hero in Jones's mould but a coolly rational man, ready to take his share of the blame but no more. Mrs Arbuthnot takes on the role of wronged innocent, thereby seeking to place the entire burden of responsibility upon Lord Illingworth and to keep Gerald to herself. In their encounter at the end of Act II, Lord Illingworth undercuts the role she adopts, neither accusing nor justifying but answering her declarations with calm common sense. Similarly, when she tells her son the sad and cliché-ridden tale of an innocent maiden tricked out of her virtue by the dastardly Lord Illingworth, Gerald denies her claim to absolute moral superiority just as effectively as his father does, answering: 'I dare say the girl was just as much to blame as Lord Illingworth was.—After all, would a really nice girl, a girl with any nice feelings at all, go away from her home with a man to whom she was not married, and live with him as his wife?' Mrs Arbuthnot's real triumph is that she finally goads Lord Illingworth into acting out precisely the role in which she has all along sought to cast him: when she tells him he has lost Gerald for ever, Lord Illingworth retaliates in the caddish style of the traditional villain, addressing her as 'one's mistress and one's—', thereby earning his dismissal as 'A man of no importance.'

The transformation of Lord Illingworth and Mrs Arbuthnot from the wicked aristocrat and seduced maiden of traditional melodrama into the more complex and ambiguous characters of the final version transforms the play from a simple struggle between good and evil into a more realistic and intricate struggle between two individuals. In the early manuscript version Mrs Arbuthnot's battle to keep hold of her son is presented as the struggle of the virtuous against the corrupt, much like that of Mrs Gaskell's Ruth, who rejected marriage to her seducer, declaring forthrightly: 'You shall have nothing to do with my boy, by my consent, much less by my agency. I would rather see him working on the roadside than leading such a life— being such a one as you are.' So, in the autograph manuscript, Lord Illingworth seeks to make a disciple of Gerald and to undermine his mother's influence, while Mrs Arbuthnot represents a strong but charitable morality. In the final version the moral conflict between villain and heroine is less clearly defined. ⟨. . .⟩

Gerald Arbuthnot is by contrast little more than a stage prop in the confrontation between his parents. Beyond the minimal attributes of naïvety and boyish enthusiasm, he is virtually characterless. Indeed, Wilde deliberately reduced Gerald to a cipher. In the earlier manuscript versions he is equally innocuous but he is at least possessed of his own minimal moral sense; he is capable of being influenced and corrupted, whereas the final Gerald jumps from one posture to another without ever expressing a viewpoint at all. So, in the autograph manuscript, Gerald is attracted by his father's philosophy, remarking to his mother: 'I suppose you think him bad because he doesn't believe all the old conventionalities one has been taught about life. He is perfectly right. There is not one of them that is not unsound, illogical, ridiculous.' In this version, Hester and Mrs Arbuthnot win Gerald back to their absolute morality by presenting themselves as victims of Lord Illingworth's villainous advances, but the play still ends with a darker hint that Gerald will never again be the same artless innocent. Having been struck in the face by Mrs Arbuthnot, Lord Illingworth departs after one final thrust: 'You are the woman whom I did the honour of asking to be my wife. How foolish the wisest of us are at times. But someday your son may call you by a worse name. He has my blood in his veins as well as yours.' It is doubtful whether the final Gerald Arbuthnot has any blood running in his veins at all. It is the unmarried mother who hogs the limelight, while the illegitimate son is consigned to the wings.

—Sos Eltis, *Revising Wilde: Society and Subversion in the Plays of Oscar Wilde* (Oxford, England: Clarendon Press, 1996): pp. 116–119.

⟨ℬ⟩

Neil Sammells: A Perfect Act

[Neil Cameron Sammells is the Dean of Humanities and Reader in English at Bath College of Higher Education, England. In addition to *Wilde Style: The Plays and Prose of Oscar Wilde* (2000), he has written *Tom Stoppard: The Artist as Critic,* and co-edited *Irish Writing: Exile and Subversion, Writing and Censorship in Britain,* and *Writing and America.* He is also author of numerous articles and reviews, and is the co-editor of *Irish Studies Review.* This selection discusses Wilde's notorious disregard of plot in favor of developments of character and language.]

That *A Woman of No Importance,* which opened on 19 April 1893, was in some respects a deliberate attempt to outdo its predecessor, is clear in Wilde's claim to Gilbert Burgess that he wrote the first act 'in answer to the critics who said that *Lady Windermere's Fan* lacked action. In the act in question there was absolutely no action at all. It was a perfect act.' The remark signals, in part, Wilde's oft-proclaimed lack of interest in plot: the significant events in *A Woman of No Importance* amount to little more than an off-stage attempt at a kiss in Act Three and the final sensational moment when the puritan, Mrs Arbuthnot, outstrips Lady Windermere and her fan, and strikes Lord Illingworth across the face with his glove. This is a play in which talk all but entirely displaces action, as Wilde constructs a dramatic dialogue characterized by the constant undercutting of sentimental puritan rhetoric and the mannered, competitive flirtation between the two dandies, Lord Illingworth and Mrs Allonby. It is also a 'perfect act' in another sense. In that anticipation of postmodernity's denial of the distinction between the natural and the cultural which we have already noted, and examined in Wilde's enculturation of the natural world in the artful opening to *Dorian Gray*, in *A Woman of No Importance* the 'real', the simple and the genuine are cancelled by the artificial, the sophisticated and the theatrical. Philip Prowse's acclaimed 1991 production—which rescued this least-performed of Wilde's society comedies from relative obscurity—accentuated this aspect of the play in its mannerist approach to the text. Prowse's staging of Wilde's 'perfect act' began as the audience was still taking its seats in the auditorium and the luche young aristocrat Lord Alfred played a game of barefoot croquet. The opening exchanges between Sir John, Lady Caroline and Hester Worsley took place as they strolled in front of an eighteenth-century-style landscape painting in a huge gilt frame. The stage was dominated by a lily pond and ornamental urns. According to Robert Gordon, Prowse's design was of an English countryside 'completely landscaped, nature transformed utterly into art.' At the opening of Act Two, the curiously upholstered lily pond was transformed—entirely in keeping with the logic of Wilde's play—into a massive round sofa covered in artfully clashing striped, spotted and checked fabrics and giant cushions in eye-bruishing colours. The exterior landscape painting was replaced as a backdrop by a wooden, gold 'curtain'. In the final act, the landscape of Hunstanton Chase in Act One could be seen through the windows of Mrs Arbuthnot's house with its minimalist décor and deep blue curtains.

What Prowse, as director and designer, had recognized was that Wilde's play like so much of his other work, deploys the distinction between the natural and the artificial only to deny to it. The distinction is established in the opening dialogue between Lady Caroline and Hester. The young American (played by a black actress in Prowse's production, to emphasize her 'separateness') is asked if she has ever stayed in an English country house before. When she says that she has not, Lady Caroline asks, 'Have you any country? What we should call country?' Hester replies 'We have the largest country in the world, Lady Caroline. They used to tell us at school that some of our states are as big as France and England put together'. What Lady Caroline would call country is glaringly there for all to see and is a neat cancellation of Hester's rather smug faith in the great outdoors: 'You must find it very draughty', she says. As the play progresses, Hester's attachment to the 'natural world' becomes synonymous with a naïve belief in the pure, the authentic, the unspoiled. Gerald Arbuthnot, she announces, 'has a beautiful nature! He is so simple, so sincere. He has one of the most beautiful natures I have ever come across'. In the second act, she interrupts the cynical observations of the aristocratic women on men in general, and husbands in particular, by announcing that American society consists 'simply of all the good women and good men we have in our country.' 'What is that dreadful girl talking about?' asks Mrs Allonby. 'She is painfully natural, is she not?' comes Lady Stutfield's reply. However, Hester's understanding of what is natural, and the values she attaches to it, is repeatedly undercut. Lady Hunstanton recalls that Lord Illingworth balked at marrying Lady Kelso because her family was too large (or was it her feet?), though she would have made an excellent ambassador's wife. Lady Caroline agrees that 'She certainly has a wonderful facility of remembering people's names, and forgetting people's faces.' 'Well, that,' responds Lady Hunstanton mysteriously, 'is very natural'. Mrs Allonby sweeps in and compliments the hostess on her wonderful trees, 'But somehow, I feel sure that if I lived in the country for six months, I should become so unsophisticated that no one would take the slightest notice of me.' 'I assure you dear,' says Lady Hunstanton, recalling the elopement of Lady Belton and Lord Feathersdale which prompted the former's husband to die of joy, or gout, 'that the country has not that effect at all'. The exchange neatly cancels that literary distinction between the innocent countryside and the wicked town which Wilde was to subject to further comic deconstruction in *The Importance of Being Earnest.*

Lord Illingworth's entrance in the first act signals a further rejection of Hester's notions about the natural. He immediately detaches the signifier 'America' from the signifieds Hester cements it to and so claims for herself: candour, simplicity, genuineness, moral straightforwardness. 'The youth of America is their oldest tradition,' he observes, after a few derogatory remarks about its literary achievements, 'It has been going on now for three hundred years. To hear them talk one would imagine they were in their first childhood. As far as civilisation goes they are in the second.' But this is not mere xenophobia. His contempt for the politically-correct MP, Kelvil (who is preparing a speech on what is no doubt Hester's favourite subject, Purity), is palpable, as it is for the concatenation of 'natural', 'health' and 'Englishness'. 'Health', he opines, is the silliest word in our language, 'and one knows so well the popular idea of health. The English country gentleman galloping after a fox—the unspeakable in full pursuit of the uneatable'. He and Mrs Allonby are hot-house flowers. She tells Lady Hunstanton that she will take a walk as far as the conservatory: 'Lord Illingworth told me this morning that there was an orchid there as beautiful as the seven deadly sins.' Mrs Arbuthnot, on the other hand, associates herself with the 'natural simplicity' Hester so approves of. 'It looks quite the happy English home', notes Mrs Allonby sardonically, when she enters Mrs Arbuthnot's house in the final act. Lady Hunstanton points out that 'Most women in London, nowadays, seem to furnish their rooms with nothing but orchids, foreigners and French novels. But here we have the room of a sweet saint. Fresh natural flowers, books that don't shock one, pictures that one can look at without blushing'. 'But I like blushing,' says Mrs Allonby. 'Well, there *is* a good deal to be said for blushing,' confesses Lady Hunstanton, 'if one can do it at the right moment'. What is clear is that the visitors from Hunstanton Chase allow of no such thing as a natural reaction. To them all behaviour is studied, mannnered, part of the social language of flirtation, control, power. Everything is in scare quotes. They also recognize that Mrs Arbuthnot is carefully designing her own stage-set in which she can play the starring role of penitent sinner. Indeed, she possesses an admirable theatrical sense. Her first entrance '*from the terrace behind with a lace veil over her head*' is artfully timed to coincide with the climax of Hester's tirade against sexual misdemeanour in Act Two: 'Let all women who have sinned be punished.' Mrs Arbuthnot's is indeed a perfect act.

—Neil Sammells, *Wilde Style: The Plays and Prose of Oscar Wilde* (England: Pearson Education Limited, 2000): pp. 91–93.

Works by
Oscar Wilde

Ravenna. 1878.

Vera, or the Nihilists. 1880.

Poems 1881.

The Duchess of Padua. 1883.

The Truth of Masks. 1885.

Lord Arthur Savile's Crime. 1887.

The Canterville Ghost. 1887.

The Sphinx Without a Secret. 1887.

The Model Millionaire. 1887.

The Happy Prince and Other Tales. 1888.

The Young King. 1888.

The Decay of Lying. 1889.

Pen, Pencil and Poison. 1889.

Symphony in Yellow. 1889.

The Birthday of the Infanta. 1889.

The Portrait of Mr. W. H. 1889.

In the Forest. 1889.

The Critic as Artist. 1890.

The Picture of Dorian Gray. 1890.

The Soul of Man Under Socialism. 1890.

Intentions. 1891.

Lord Arthur Savile's Crime and Other Stories. 1891.

A House of Pomegranates. 1891.

Lady Windermere's Fan. 1892.

Salomé. 1893.

A Woman of No Importance. 1893.

The Disciple. 1893.

The House of Judgment. 1893.

The Sphinx. 1894.

Poems in Prose. 1894.

The Florentine Tragedy. 1894.

La Sainte Courtisane. 1894.

Phrases and Philosophies for the Use of the Young. 1894.

A Few Maxims for the Instruction of the Over-Educated. 1894.

An Ideal Husband. 1895.

The Importance of Being Earnest. 1895.

De Profundis. 1897.

Two letters to *The Daily Chronicle.* 1897–1898.

The Ballad of Reading Gaol. 1898.

De Profundis. 1905. (published)

The Rise of Historical Criticism. 1905.

Collected Edition of the Works of Oscar Wilde, ed. Robert Ross. 1908.

Oscar Wilde: Art and Morality: A Defense of "The Picture of Dorian Gray," ed. Stuart Mason. 1908.

The Letters of Oscar Wilde, ed. Rupert Hart-Davis. 1962.

Complete Works of Oscar Wilde, ed. G. B. Foreman. 1966.

Literary Criticism of Oscar Wilde, ed. Stanley Weintraub. 1968.

The Artist as Critic: Critical Writings of Oscar Wilde, ed. Richard Ellmann. 1969.

The Complete Shorter Fiction of Oscar Wilde, ed. Isobel Murray. 1979.

More Letters of Oscar Wilde, ed. Rupert Hart-Davis. 1985.

Oscar Wilde's Oxford Notebooks: A Portrait of Mind in the Making, ed. Philip E. Smith II and Michael S. Helfand. 1989.

Works About
Oscar Wilde

Ackroyd, Peter. *The Last Testament of Oscar Wilde*. New York: Harper and Row, 1983.

Beckson, Karl, ed. *Oscar Wilde: The Critical Heritage*. London, England: Routledge and Kegan Paul, 1970.

Behrendt, Patricia Flanagan. *Oscar Wilde: Eros and Aesthetics*. London, England: Macmillan Academic and Professional Ltd, 1991.

Bird, Alan. *The Plays of Oscar Wilde*. London, England: Vision Press Limited, 1977.

Bloom, Harold, ed. *Oscar Wilde*. New York: Chelsea House Publishers, 1985.

———. *Oscar Wilde's* The Importance of Being Earnest. New York: Chelsea House Publishers, 1988.

Brown, Julia Prewitt. *Cosmopolitan Criticism: Oscar Wilde's Philosophy of Art*. Charlottesville, Virginia: University Press of Virginia, 1997.

Cohen, Philip K. *The Moral Vision of Oscar Wilde*. London, England: Associated University Presses, 1976.

Douglas, Alfred Lord. *Oscar Wilde: A Summing Up*. London, England: Gerald Duckworth, 1940.

Eagletown, Terry. *Saint Oscar*. Derry: Field Day, 1989.

Ellmann, Richard, ed. *The Artist as Critic: Critical Writings of Oscar Wilde*. Chicago: University of Chicago Press, 1969.

———. *Eminent Domain: Yeats Among Wilde, Joyce, Pound, Eliot, and Auden*. New York: Vintage, 1970.

———,ed. *Oscar Wilde: A Collection of Critical Essays*. Englewood Cliffs, New Jersey: Prentice Hall, 1986.

———. *Oscar Wilde*. London, England: Hamish Hamilton, 1987.

Eltis, Sos. *Revising Wilde: Society and Subversion in the Plays of Oscar Wilde*. Oxford, England: Clarendon Press, 1996.

Ericksen, Donald H. *Oscar Wilde*. Boston: Twayne, 1977.

Freedman, Jonathan, ed. *Oscar Wilde: A Collection of Critical Essays.* Upper Saddle River, New Jersey: Prentice Hall, 1996.

Gagnier, Regenia, ed. *Critical Essays on Oscar Wilde.* New York: G. K. Hall & Co., 1991.

Gide, André. *Oscar Wilde: In Memoriam.* New York: Philosophical Library, 1949.

Gillespie, Michael Patrick. *Oscar Wilde and the Poetics of Ambiguity.* Florida: University Press of Florida, 1996.

Harris, Alan. "Oscar Wilde as Playwright: A Centenary Review." *Adelphi* 30, no. 3 (1954): 212–40.

Horan, Patrick M. *The Importance of Being Paradoxical: Maternal Presence in the Works of Oscar Wilde.* London, England: Associated University Presses, 1997.

Knox, Melissa. *Oscar Wilde: A Long and Lovely Suicide.* New Haven, Connecticut: Yale University Press, 1994.

Mahaffey, Vicki. *States of Desire: Wilde, Yeats, Joyce, and the Irish Experiment.* New York: Oxford University Press, 1998.

Nassaar, Christopher S. *Into the Demon Universe: A Literary Exploration of Oscar Wilde.* New Haven, Connecticut: Yale University Press, 1974.

Nelson, Walter W. *Oscar Wilde and the Dramatic Critics: A Study in Victorian Theatre.* Lund, Sweden: Bloms Boktryckerl, 1989.

Page, Norman. *An Oscar Wilde Chronology.* London, England: Macmillan Academic and Professional Ltd, 1991.

Paglia, Camille. "Oscar Wilde and the English Epicene," *Raritan,* 4 (1985), 85–109.

Pearson, Hesketh. *The Life of Oscar Wilde.* London: Penguin, 1960.

Powell, Kerry. *Oscar Wilde and the Theatre of the 1890s.* Cambridge, England: Cambridge University Press, 1994.

Raby, Peter. *Oscar Wilde.* Cambridge, England: Cambridge University Press, 1988.

Ransome, Arthur. *Oscar Wilde: A Critical Study.* 3rd Edition. London, England: Methuen, 1913.

Roditi, Edouard. *Oscar Wilde.* New York: New Directions, 1947.

Sammells, Neil. *Wilde Style: The Plays and Prose of Oscar Wilde.* London, England: Pearson Education Limited, 2000.

San Juan, Jr., Epifanio. *The Art of Oscar Wilde.* Princeton, New Jersey: Princeton University Press, 1967.

Shewan, Rodney. *Oscar Wilde: Art and Egotism.* London, England: The Macmillan Press Ltd, 1977.

Stokes, John. *In the Nineties.* London, England: Harvester Wheatsheaf, 1989.

———. *Oscar Wilde. Myths, Miracles, and Imitations.* Cambridge, England: Cambridge University Press, 1996.

Varty, Anne. *A Preface to Oscar Wilde.* London, England: Addison Wesley Longman Limited, 1998.

Worth, Katharine. *The Irish Drama of Europe from Yeats to Beckett.* London: Athlone Press, 1978.

Index of
Themes and Ideas